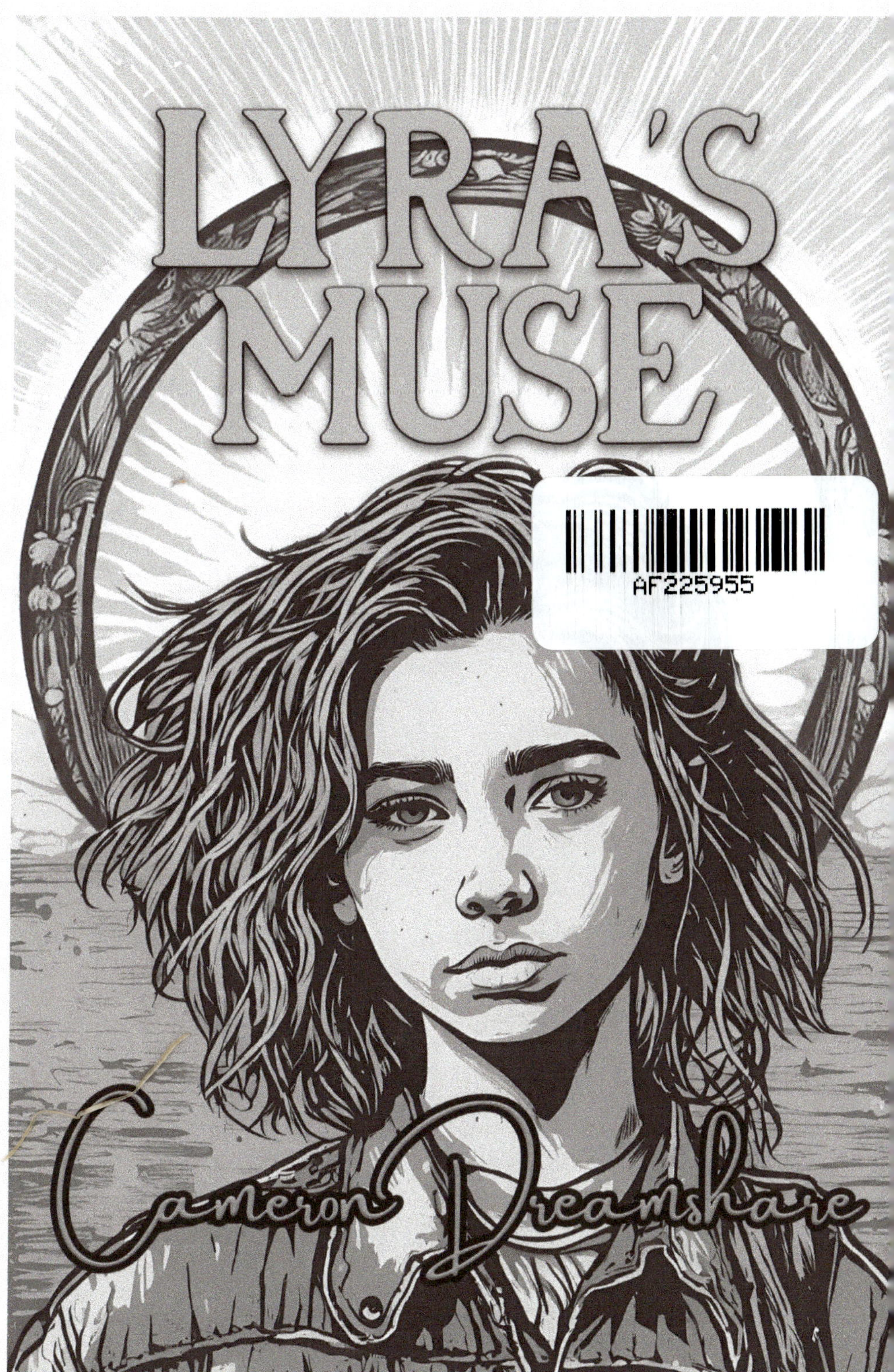
LYRA'S MUSE
Cameron Dreamshare

ISBN: 978-1-989832-12-7
Copyright 2024 by Studio Dreamshare

Studio Dreamshare Press
www.studiodreamshare.com
For more information and permission, contact:
studiodreamshare@gmail.com

CHAPTER 1: Lyra

Lyra drew her black hoodie closed at the neck with one hand as she ducked into shadows behind the large grey box building. With her other hand she dragged a bucket of cement. She looked all around her and listened hard. She saw no one, heard nothing, and felt no tingle of being observed. Downtown in the cities, drones buzzed everywhere, watching, but out here there was nothing— and no one— worth monitoring.

Lyra pulled out a bent old spatula from inside her sweater. She dipped it into the cement-like mixture in the bucket, getting a large glob. As she lifted it to the wall, a shiver of excitement coursed through her. This was her first big mural, and her first time using this technique on a building. She spread the goo in a large area as high as she could reach, patting it into cracks and crevices, preparing her surface.

Lyra started drawing on the walls of their trailer when she was nine. She used charred remains from oil drum fires. Her mother was angry when she drew at home so she had to sneak out and find walls and pavement where no one would mind. The drawings were harmless scribbles that just washed away anyway. Lyra wished she had pencils and paints but they couldn't afford any.

She reached into her pocket and drew out a bag full of ground up charcoal and ashes. She used her hands to apply it to the cement paste, first frowning as she patted clumsily and then grinning as she got used to the technique.

"It works," she whispered to herself triumphantly.

The technique was inspired by an old tattered book Lyra nabbed when the public library closed down. She didn't understand all the vocabulary, but she figured out the gist of it. The ancients did something called a fresco where they created an image directly into drying plaster on a wall. Lyra used charcoal and ashes to create lines and shadows instead of powdered pigment.

An image began to form beneath her fast-moving hands. It was a woman with long hair, high-chiselled cheek bones and her hands open. Lyra reached into her pocket and grabbed a glass jar with a special yellow mixture inside. Lyra had harvested the first dandelions, crushing their golden juices into watered-down cement in an old jar along with anything else she could find that was yellow. She even scraped yellow paint off the crumbling road and ground it up painstakingly to brighten her concoction. She beamed with triumph as she coloured a glowing halo around the woman's head with pigment she had invented herself. She stood back to admire her work. She flicked on her device, only for a brief instant to save the battery, and compared the drawing to a picture of the real Joan Whiteduck.

"Not bad," she murmured. The likeness was there.

Lyra stepped forward and wrote "Praise" in stylized script across the halo. It was a pun. The woman's name was "Joan", pronounced the same as *jaune*, the French word for yellow. Lyra was a habitante, a French-ancestry

New Englander.

I wonder if anyone will get it, she thought.

Lyra was only twelve years old, but she was already smarter than most, if not all, of the adults in her life. Despite her smarts she did not realize this yet, and just accepted that she was strange.

Suddenly, she heard a noise nearby. She hastily dipped the spatula in the bucket of thick cement again and applied a glob below the drawing. She carved out *MUSE,* her signature.

When she was little, she signed her drawings 'Lyra Muse'. When she started writing on walls, she dropped 'Lyra' so she wouldn't get caught. Lyra was her given name, Muse was not. Her mother, Sayre, used to change her last name every time she had a new boyfriend, and she never bothered to tell Lyra hers. Lyra didn't really have a last name so she named herself.

Lyra heard the scrape of a shoe on the pavement in the darkness and she instinctively jumped away, but it was too late. A hand snaked out and grabbed her arm with an iron grip. She turned to see the large hand on her and followed the arm up to the man's face. He looked angry.

"The fuck you doin?" he seemed to growl at her.

"I… I'm sorry…" she stuttered, her eyes searching wildly for an escape.

"I should beat some sense into you," he snarled, shaking her.
Lyra's hood fell down around her shoulders and she looked up at him with large terrified eyes.

The man's brow unfurrowed and his fear melted. She was just a little girl. He looked at the spatula in her hand and then at the figure on the wall. It was a young woman. A yellow sun blazed around her head like a halo. It was pretty good.

The man looked back at the little girl.

"Please don't wreck my drawing," whispered Lyra fiercely.

The man looked from Lyra back to the drawing and back to Lyra again. He let go of her arm and roared with laughter, slapping his hands together for effect.

"Bravo!" he said with a big grin.

"That's French," said Lyra in her soft voice.

"Bien sûr," he replied.

"Ma famille… est un peu française…" she said slowly.

Papa Gilles spoke a kind of American Franglais— English with a French accent and peppered with French words and phrases. Her mother, Sayre, had all but lost it. Lyra could speak a little.

"And what should I do with you?" asked the man. The words were serious but the edge was gone from his voice.

Lyra relaxed.

"Well I was just drawing Joan Whiteduck…" fumbled Lyra.

"I know what you were doing," said the man. "You're an artiste."

Lyra was silent. No one had ever called her that before. She liked how it sounded.

"This here's pretty good," he said.

Joan Whiteduck was a teenage environmental activist who was big on the news.

"Thanks."

"I'm Basquiat," said the man, holding out his hand.

Lyra took it and shook it. It was her first handshake.

"Nice to meet you," she said.

Then she took off as fast as she could.

"Hey, you forgot your bucket, MUSE," said Basquiat, laughing as she disappeared into the darkness of night.

Lyra lived with Sayre, Brandon, and Papa Gilles in Dummer Mobile Home Park. It was a village of about 40 trailers and a labyrinth of adjoining sheds and structures where she had grown up. When she got home, she stashed the cement-encrusted spatula under the trailer and went inside.

Her brother Brandon snored softly on the couch in the main area wrapped in a dirty yellow sheet. Lyra slipped past him into the back where she and her mother Sayre slept. To her dismay, there was a man who stunk of cigarettes sprawled out in the bed. Lyra recognized his face but she'd never seen him here in her home before.

She looked at him, sweaty in her bed, one arm flung proprietarily over her mother who was curled up against him. Lyra frowned and backed out. She went back into the main area, past her brother and into the front compartment of the trailer. She would rather sleep with Papa Gilles than Sayre and a strange man. She would never sleep by Brandon. She hated him.

Lyra slipped into the corner of the bed where Gilles was snoring heavily. Papa Gilles was not Lyra's father, or Brandon's either. Some people thought he was Sayre's father, and she never corrected them.

He wasn't.

Sayre used to live in a nearby city called Goreham. That's where she had Brandon, and where bad things happened to her. Somehow she hooked up with Papa Gilles who took them into his trailer in hard times. Gilles was a lot older than Sayre and though at first he tried to have a relationship with her, he could tell she was just sleeping with him for a place to stay with the child. Eventually he relented and Sayre moved into the back sleeping area with Brandon. Times were good for a while, but when things got hard again she turned tricks for cash. At some point Sayre was pregnant again and no one was sure if the father was one of her deadbeat boyfriends or a Jon. They all knew it wasn't Gilles'. Lyra was born, and Papa Gilles turned out to be as much a father to her as Sayre was a mother.

Lyra curled up into a ball at the corner of Gilles' bed like a woodland creature. He didn't move. She drifted off to sleep dreaming of Joan Whiteduck.

The next day Lyra awoke to the sound of shouts and the drone of motorcycle engines. She sat up and rubbed her eyes.

Papa Gilles groaned.

"Shut yer goddamn racket, calisse!" he shouted from his grimy pillows. He rolled over and noticed Lyra there at the end of his bed.

"Good morning Pap," she said sleepily.

"Good morning mousie," he said. "What are you doing in here?"

"Sayre has a guest…"

"I see."

Papa Gilles grumbled incoherently to himself as he strained to get up, rubbing his knees. He swung his legs over the side of the bed.

"You okay?" asked Lyra.

"Oh fine," he replied.

Papa Gilles had polio as a child and his family couldn't afford the expensive hospital fees for treatment. He was lucky to be alive. He suffered from joint pain and a severe limp ever since.

"Sayre!" he shouted out across the trailer. "Get some goddamn coffee on!"

The motorcycles droned closer. Something was going on outside.

Lyra went into the main area of the trailer and peered out the little window.

"The Dummer Boyz," she said quietly.

Brandon jumped up from the couch and pushed her aside to look. Lyra resisted the urge to rub her arm where he'd pushed her too hard.

Sayre came into the main area followed by the strange man.

"Stay outta sight," she said.

The Dummer Boyz were a local gang out of Dummer, New Hampshire who were trying to run the show. They paid tribute to the Prince of Coos County, Banger Jones, who was a member of the Rebels responsible for this area. He exacted tribute from all the little gangs and paid off the Fraternity. A few years ago the Dummer Boyz challenged the Rebels and a small 'war' ensued, but the Rebels won soundly with their weaponized forces and put the Dummer Boyz down. Now the Boyz were proud goonies for the Rebels' cause.

"Get out of the window," said Sayre.

"Eff off," said Brandon to his mother, continuing to watch from the window.

She tutted but said nothing.

Further up the muddy trail between the shelters, where the "nicer" vehicle-buildings were, Mustang Dougie squeezed out of his large trailer. His sweaty face was red with effort as he walked his girth slowly into the clearing outside his home. He was the unofficial leader of Dummer Mobile Home Park. He had been an executive in a large American manufacturing company that went under years ago, so off the highway into Dummer he had a large warehouse half-full of coveted imported goods like chips and candy bars that he used for barters and bribes.

"Dougie!" shouted Rusty, the head of the Dummer Boyz, hopping off his motorcycle. "What do you have for us today?"

Several gang members left their bikes and walked up and down the rows of trailers, peering into windows, leering at the wary people inside.

Dougie licked his lips, rustling open the decrepit plastic bag hanging off his fat arm. It was onions.

"Enough of that shit," said Rusty. "What are we going to do with that?" he swatted the bag out of Dougie's hand. The onions scattered into the mud.

Dougie Mustang's face showed his annoyance but he didn't say a thing.

"We want some more of those chips we know you got stashed up in here," said Rusty.

"Now see, I'm running low," said Dougie, sweating

profusely.

"I know that ain't true," said Rusty, slapping Dougie's large gut. The other gang members laughed from their motorcycles. Dougie recoiled in pain.

Brandon laughed loudly from their trailer. A gang member shoved his face in the window. Sayre fell backwards clutching Lyra to her breast and hiding her pretty face. Brandon stared at the man with a mix of awe and fascination. The man laughed and continued walking. Brandon's eyes followed him hungrily.

"Aww don't be so sensitive," said the leader of the Dummer Boyz as Dougie Mustang held his stomach and moaned in pain.

"Next month we'll have it, okay? Please," said Dougie, doubled over. He needed to put on a good show for the Dummer Mobile Home Park folks watching so they wouldn't accuse him of ripping them off and give him more tribute. Each person living here paid him for paying off the Dummer Boyz, and then some.

"Go grab me what I want before I get angry," snarled Rusty. "We didn't waste this gasoline coming out here for nothing."

Gasoline was a prized commodity these days. Decades of wars with the Middle East meant that embargoes threatened the oil supply constantly. One day the pumps would be cheap as anything and the next they would cost more than the car. The American market was unstable.

Dougie Mustang sighed heavily and made a large show of hobbling and wincing back into his trailer. He pretended to dig around loudly, filling his arms with enough chips to satisfy the Dummer Boyz. He marched them out sadly and filled a battered plastic container on the small trailer pulled by motorcycles, beside the bags of tribute from other villages on their route.

"Woohoo!" The motorcycle engines revved and the

Boyz spun out of town, hooting and cursing as they left.

Papa Gilles cuffed Brandon upside the head.

"That was stupid, boy," he said.

Brandon jumped up angrily. Sayre grabbed at him.

"Baby…" she cooed, "it's okay…"

He jerked away from her and left the trailer, slamming the door behind him.

Sayre sighed. The half-clothed man behind her turned and went back to bed. Sayre followed.

"I'm going out," said Lyra to Papa Gilles.

"Okay mousie, be careful," he said, going back to bed himself.

"I will."

CHAPTER 2: Lyra

Lyra spent the day with Inas, an old woman who lived just past the edge of the trailer park. She was the only person Lyra knew who lived in a real house. It was falling apart, but it was cozy, especially in the winter when the broken down wood stove rattled out heat. Inas was eccentric, and perhaps a little senile, but she knew about gardening. She grew vegetables around her house and in secret patches in the surrounding areas. Inas had trouble walking long distances and bending over now, so Lyra helped out in exchange for food. Sayre got food for Papa Gilles and Brandon her own way.

Inas only ate real food. Lyra liked that. She enjoyed planting seeds and wondering what they were doing in there, under the soil. Sure enough, they poked out of the ground just like Inas said they would. Lyra learned about the taste of the soil, the direction of the sun, irrigation, and other secrets that the old woman revealed bit by bit as Lyra obeyed her sharp commands.

After weeding a bed far out beyond the mobile homes

beside a sluggish creek, Lyra wiped the sweat from her brow and started heading back to Inas'. It was a good hour's walk. Inas was a little paranoid, Lyra thought, but then again Lyra wasn't around when the gardens had been plundered in harder times. Inas didn't plan on starving, and she had a few mouths to feed, including Lyra's.

As the girl approached the house, she heard voices inside. She bent her knees as she walked, like a cat, ready to spring away in an instant if need be. She heard Inas' gravelly rich tones, and she heard a man as well. His voice sounded familiar but she couldn't place it. They weren't fighting; Inas was yelling at him, but only in her usual way.

Lyra peered in the window. Inas was standing at the stove, stirring her cast iron pot. She always had a soup brewing in there. The man was sitting at the table with his back to Lyra.

Suddenly Inas' eyes snapped to the window. Lyra cursed under her breath. Nothing got past Inas.

"Get in here," said the old woman. Lyra could hear her through the window. She scampered over to the door. There was no use in disobeying.

Lyra pushed open the door a crack, peering in. The man turned slowly and their eyes locked.

He roared with laughter. Lyra recognized his laugh; it was the man from the box building the other night, the one who caught her painting. She was ready to bolt.

Inas' eyes lit up at the sound of his laugh and she joined in. Lyra stared in fascination. Inas' laugh was beautiful and she didn't hear it often. She scooted in, closing the door behind her.

"It's the artiste," said the man.

What was his name again? thought Lyra. *Oh… that's right… Basquiat.*

"Come sit," said Inas.

Lyra sat down across the table from Basquiat. He smiled at her, genuinely pleased to see her again. She felt the same but her face was mostly always serious.

Inas brought Lyra a bowl of soup. She leaned over it, blowing it cool, and quietly she reported the state of the garden to Inas.

"So you're the one who's been helping her out," said Basquiat. "She was letting on she was doing everything herself but I knew someone must have been around."

Inas took his empty bowl and filled it up with a second helping.

"Come sit with us," he said to the old woman.

"Well I guess I will," she said.

Lyra was surprised, since Inas never seemed to listen to anyone. Inas looked at her expression and laughed.

"Don't go looking at me like that," she said. "Bas is my best friend Violet's son. He's family."

Violet had died of cancer a few years back. Basquiat reached out and squeezed Inas' hand.

"So how do you two know each other?" he asked.

Lyra and Inas looked at each other. To any old person it looked like a casual glance, but Bas could see affection passing between two strong people with the same kind of grit.

"We just do is all," said Lyra. She was annoyed because her voice came out like a whisper. She had no control over it. She was shy.

"You look well fed," said Inas, turning to Bas. "I guess you're not doing too bad up there."

"Things are going great," he said. "All my dreams are coming true Auntie…" his eyes lit up with excitement. "It's a work in progress, but the Androscoggin Free Zone is becoming a reality."

Inas snorted.

"Finish your soup young man."

"What's that?" asked Lyra quietly. Her interest was piqued.

"We're building a Free Zone. There's a group of us… do you know about the Free Zones?"

Lyra shook her head. She didn't know much about anything. But she was keen to learn.

"Every Free Zone is different, but basically all over
the country people are declaring autonomy from the
government. They're not doing anything for us anyway,
spending all our money on weapons and wars... so we're
breaking free and drawing new borders and living in the
new way, our own way..."

"Sounds like the Dummer Boyz," said Lyra quietly.

Basquiat was silent for a second.

"You're right. They don't care for the government
either. Those guys are why we need good people to
set up good ways, because we can't just let those evil
bastards take over."

Inas made a scolding sound.

"Sorry for cursing," said Bas.

"So how do you do that?" asked Lyra.

"We're reclaiming abandoned places and fixing
them up for the community to use properly, making sure
everybody has good food, education, art... we have rules
so that everything is fair. We make the rules together."

Lyra was intrigued. She also liked how he didn't talk
to her like a baby.

"So far we reclaimed the old Megamart and now it's
a marketplace, hostel, jam space, library, garden... it's
just the beginning but it's something great, I can feel it.
Right in that building you painted on," he laughed.

Inas cackled along with him.

Lyra's eyes smiled.

"How did you get up there, anyway?" he asked
her, realizing that she must live close by here at Inas'.
There was no public transit anymore, the counties were
too poor. It was a four or five hour walk from there to
Dummer. He knew because he had just done it for his
visit.

"Bike," she said, after a moment of hesitation. Lyra's
second most prized possession, after her art kit, was
her bicycle. It was an old bike that one of Papa Gilles'
buddies tuned up for her. She didn't advertise that she
had one though. She walked everywhere close by and

the bicycle was mainly for her art missions. She usually explored at night, and she avoided other people. People could always be dangerous. She zipped over to the ghostly stretch of abandoned box store buildings perfect for her murals in just over an hour, did her work, and zipped back. Her family had no idea.

"Nice."

"Are there… artists… in the Free Zone?" asked Lyra.

"Yea. We've got artists, musicians, performers of all kinds. You could come check it out."

Maybe I will, thought Lyra.

"Maybe when you're a little older… how old are you anyway? It's seventeen and up at the Megamart. At the Free Zone I mean… still getting used to the name change."

Lyra just looked at him with big round eyes, betraying no emotion. She said nothing.

I'm twelve, she thought. But she wasn't telling him that.

"Well I'm glad to see someone's helping out my Auntie," he said.

"Especially since I don't see enough of you," said Inas.

"Don't worry, I'm working on a cozy little spot for you in the Free Zone," he said.

Lyra was sad at the thought of Inas leaving her house.

"Ha," said Inas, feeling the same.

"I'd love you to come teach our people about gardening," said Bas. "I've started with what you taught me but there's so much I don't know. And I worry about you up here… your safety… You never know, living so close to these white folks."

Lyra didn't say anything. She knew exactly what he meant. She had seen and heard terrible things. It wasn't just the scary men. Sayre, her own mother, said awful things about black people. Even now, Lyra felt some fear sitting across the table from Basquiat. She knew with a deep awareness that that wasn't fair. She was good at reading people and she could tell from his energy and his interaction with Inas that this man was caring, funny, and smart. She remembered holding Inas' warm and wrinkled old hand for the first time, realizing that black people were just people like everybody else, and Inas was special because she was special, and Lyra loved her. She pushed her feelings of acculturated intimidation aside. Basquiat was Inas' family, and her friend now too.

"You just finish up your soup," said Inas. "And don't wait so long to come see me."

Bas laughed.

Lyra made her way home. It was still early, but she wanted to read some more of her art book and she forgot it at home. She picked her way through ditches and over the highway with grass growing tall through the large cracks in the pavement. The roads were mostly no longer used for residential cars, but she did have to keep her eyes out for the occasional transport truck or military vehicle. The rich still needed their deliveries, and drones couldn't carry everything. Above all, she listened for the whine of motorcycles. The Dummer Boyz were dangerous. When she was ten, Lyra had dropped into the ditch and lay there holding her breath for an hour after a fleet of them whizzed by her. She was sure they saw her and she was lucky that they had somewhere to be that day or else who knows what would have happened to her.

Old car wrecks and random piles of plastic trash by the roadside meant she was getting closer to Dummer Mobile Home Park. She picked up her pace, thinking of her book.

From the direction of Dummer, a figure walked toward her. He was ribby and thin, with long limbs and wide shoulders, thick brown hair on his head and none on his chin. It was a boy on the brink of shooting up into a large man. It was her brother, Brandon.

"Hey Dirt," he shouted. He called her that because her hands were always dirty from drawing or gardening.

His were just as dirty, but it still annoyed Lyra when he said it. Her back tensed up. She wanted to avoid him but there was no way now. She could tell that he was in a nasty mood, and he would bug her all the way home. She breathed in sharply and prepared to ignore him as best she could.

"Whatcha got there?" he said as he got closer, slowing his leggy stride to match hers. He made a swipe at her bag. She gripped it hard for a second and then let go. It was easier that way.

Brandon rifled through the bag roughly.

Thank goodness I didn't bring my book today, she thought.

"Vegetables," he scoffed. "Gross." He pulled out a spring onion and bit into it. He grimaced and spit it onto the ground.

Lyra clenched her jaw and said nothing.

Brandon handed the bag back. Lyra grabbed it. Brandon didn't let go.

Lyra's face betrayed annoyance. Brandon saw it and grinned. He yanked the bag away and let the vegetables scatter onto the ground.

Lyra sighed with exasperation and dropped to her knees to pick them up.

I feel like Dougie Mustang, she thought. At least he didn't punch me in the stomach.

Brandon crowed with glee. This was just the reaction he was looking for. He was desperate for attention.

"You should find something productive to do, Brandon," she said.

"What's that supposed to mean?" he snapped. He was sure she was insulting him but he didn't know what she meant.

Lyra said nothing. She stuffed the remaining veggies into the bag and kept walking.

"What's that supposed to mean?" he repeated, following after her.

She glowered but kept walking with her mouth set in

a firm line.

"Look at me when I'm talking to you!" he said, grabbing her arm roughly. It was a familiar spot, already bruised. His grip was hard.

Lyra yelped and swung out with her other arm, hitting him in the chest. She wasn't a fighter and she didn't want to hurt him, just make him go away, so the swat was weak.

Brandon snarled angrily and knocked her to the ground, sitting on her chest as she struggled to get free. Brandon laughed triumphant.

"I got you!" he said.

Lyra's head was reeling and she could see stars. The hard fall and his sudden weight knocked the wind out of her. She gasped for breath.

Brandon craved more of a reaction than he was getting. His hand darted forward and he gave her nipple a twist. The look of panic on her face was perfect. She coughed and spluttered, writhing to get free and still unable to breathe properly. She let out a guttural scream that sounded like an animal caught in a trap.

Brandon jumped up and looked around.

"Shut up," he said.

He walked off quickly.

Lyra stood up slowly, brushing herself off. When she had regained her breath, she continued on her way home.

By the time Lyra reached the Park, it was late but it felt earlier because the days were still warm and long. Papa Gilles was out front of the trailer, heating up beans on the fire. The cookstove in the trailer needed gas to run and they were all out. Some people had solar panels hooked into their setup but Gilles never was skilled in electrical. Cooking outside suited him just fine, especially when the weather was beautifully warm. Winter was always trickier. He made a "barbeque" out of an old oil tank and Sayre could cook just about anything they would ever eat on it.

"Hey mousie," he said, poking at the bean can with a stick.

"Hey Pap," said Lyra, sitting down beside him.

Sayre came out of the trailer with bowls. The half-clothed man seemed to be gone, and so did Brandon. Lyra frowned.

Good riddance to both of them, she thought.

"Have you ever heard of Free Zones?" asked Lyra.

"What are you on about?" asked Gilles. He spent most nights playing cards with his buddies and sometimes they cranked on the old TV. He had seen some talk of Free Zones in the news, but he didn't really know what it was.

"Free Zones… it's like a village where everyone takes care of each other," said Lyra quietly. "You know, properly and all that."

"Little smartie," he said, patting her head.

"She should get an education, Sayre," he said, turning to her mother. Occasionally he would say things like that, but he never helped get her anywhere so Lyra gave up hope of it long ago. There were private schools, but only for kids in rich enclaves.

"I'm homeschooling them," said Sayre.

"I know, I know," said Gilles. He knew that Lyra spent her days out running the roads. He knew she had eaten only a handful of meals with them over the last year. She was doing pretty good taking care of herself.

"Scoot," said Sayre, motioning for Gilles and Lyra to move out of the way so she could get the bean can out of the fire and fill the bowls. Papa Gilles couldn't manage it. The polio had crippled his hands in such a way that any task involving dexterity was difficult. Children around the mobile home park would occasionally taunt him. They called him "Lobster" because his hands were twisted like pincers. He was plenty strong still though and he would swiftly grab one and give them a good shake, and they would lay off him.

"Where's Brandon?" asked Gilles.

Sayre shrugged.

When Sayre and Gilles were done their beans, Sayre went back into the trailer to clean up and get ready for the night.

"So where did you get to today?" he asked.

Lyra had learned to mostly just tell him what she thought he wanted to hear. If she told him she went too far he would try to stop her from going, and if she told him about Brandon he wouldn't do anything about it. After all, how did Brandon get that way?

"I visited Inas," she said.

He nodded and poked the fire.

"I like the woods," she said after a while. "I don't like how all the trees are hacked up around here."

All the last trees around Dummer Mobile Home Park had been stripped of bark and mostly cut down by folks making cooking fires. Long ago there had been rules about cutting the trees, but a few hard winters bent the rules and that was it. Everyone ignored the rules now.

"You be careful going so far out on your own," he said.

"I know. I can't stand being cooped up here. One day I want to live in the forest," she said.

Papa Gilles scoffed. "That's not a real forest."

Lyra looked at him. She didn't know what he meant.

"Where I grew up, in White Mountain National Forest… that's a real forest."

"Tell me again about what it was like," said Lyra.

"There were trees so big you couldn't reach around them with your arms."

Lyra could only imagine such a thing. There were no trees like that around here.

"When you stood in the forest, all quiet like, you could hear a hundred different kinds of birds singing all at once."

Lyra closed her eyes and tried to imagine it.

"All with different voices, singing the same song."

Lyra sighed.

"There were animals, and a river to fish in, and all kinds of berries and such to eat, just free for the taking."

"Can we go there?" she asked, not for the first time. "It isn't that far."

"Well it's far enough," said Papa Gilles. "But… I dream of going back now and again. Before I'm too old."

Lyra frowned. She didn't think of Papa Gilles as too old to travel, but she knew he felt a lot of pain he didn't talk about.

"We could go, you and me," said Lyra softly. "I'm big enough now, and I've got the bike. We could carry what we need with us."

Gilles was quiet. Lyra could see the wheels in his head turning. She felt a blossom of hope unfurl inside her.

"Maybe Brandon should come, mousie," said Papa Gilles. "I'm not as strong as I used to be." He held up his polio-seized hands.

"No!" said Lyra. "No, please, Papa… not Brandon." Papa Gilles was silent for a while.

"You'll have to help me a lot then mousie," he said.

"I will! I'll do everything Papa Gilles. Please. I promise!"

"Well let me think on it," he said.

By that time the fire had burned down. The sun was gone and the lights of a trailer down the mud road flicked on. Lyra knew what that meant.

"Alright. Go on to bed now," he said, getting up slowly and stretching out his stiff back.

Lyra looked at him expectantly. He followed her into the trailer and tucked her in and kissed her goodnight. She was as mature as anything, but she was still twelve years old.

Gilles hobbled off down the road toward the lights. There was a crude wooden painted sign outside that read "The Pickled Peach". It was his buddy's trailer. That was where Gilles spent most nights, drinking hooch made from canned peach juice and playing cards with the old gaffers.

That night Lyra dreamed of White Mountain National Forest. She had been dreaming of it all her life, fantasizing about it from snippets of stories from Papa Gilles, but tonight it felt closer than ever. She always knew in her heart that she would make it some day, and now it seemed that time was coming.

CHAPTER 3: Lyra

"Now is the perfect time to go on our adventure," said Lyra over breakfast. They were sitting on old plastic chairs outside the trailer in the early summer sunshine, eating spring onions and eggs fried up in a cast iron skillet over Papa Gilles' BBQ.
Brandon was still nowhere to be seen.

"Well you're not wrong…" said Gilles. The weather was great for traveling.

"What are you two up to?" said Sayre, coming out of the trailer in her silk robe. The new man was with her. It appeared that he had found her again last night after all.

"Mousie wants to go to White Mountain, where I grew up," said Gilles.

"Oh yea? You seriously thinking of going?" said Sayre, lighting a cigarette hand-rolled with sumac leaves. She took a couple puffs and passed it around.

"Well I haven't had fresh trout in years," he said, mimicking a fishing gesture with his hands.

Suddenly a neighbour came over.

"Just heard that your kid was spotted riding with the
Dummer Boyz," he said, joining the circle to share the
cigarette.

"My baby!" said Sayre, alarmed. "He's too young for
all that!"

"Dumbass," said Gilles. "What should we do?"

Sayre looked at Gilles, and then at the man behind
her. She was already accepting the inevitability of the
situation.

"Well if you two go to White Mountain, I'll still have
Jeremiah to make sure I'm okay." The man behind her
shifted from one foot to the other.

Lyra felt a shudder of foreboding. She wondered if
Sayre would take her daughter running off with the same
defeat. Probably.

Aren't you going to stop Brandon? thought Lyra,
even though she hated him. She realized even as she
thought it that Brandon was probably better off with the
Boyz. He was a little thief, and one of these days he
was going to get caught by the wrong person. He was
probably better off stealing for the Boyz. They would
have his back.

"Well now mousie, it looks like this might really
happen."

The family made plans for White Mountain and
avoided talking about Brandon.

There was a knock on the trailer door. The knob
turned itself and a head popped in. It was a man in long
black robes and a stiff white collar.

"Ned!" said Papa Gilles.

"Just checking in on you," said the man.

Ned was a Care Pastor. Unlike most countries, the
USA did not have a healthcare system. They relied on
a capitalist market of medical firms selling a variety of
medical products and services. At the outset this meant a
diversity of options at reasonable prices, but eventually,
because capitalism functions through exploitation,
giant monopolies arose. Private organizations funded

all the schools, all the public works, and the delivery of healthcare too. Instead of a healthcare system, they had Big Pharma. All these so-called charity hospitals were set up by the Care Movement. It was a large organization run at the bottom by volunteers and at the top by mob bosses. When these hospitals were being built, the government welcomed them. They called it "trickle-down economics", which meant that they thought rich people would eventually share their wealth and help the needy, like these free hospitals. However, the Care Movement was a business like any other, and they established a monopoly on healthcare and the distribution of pharmacare drugs. The people at the top knew how it worked; at the bottom, Care Pastors like Ned were true believers and committed their lives to service. Ned was sent to Care Seminary to train as a pharmacist and a pastor.

"Sorry to come in at breakfast time," said Ned.

"Yea right," cackled Gilles. "You were looking for a meal, weren't you?"

Ned grinned. "Well I wouldn't say no to a bite to eat." He came inside and sat on the edge of the seat at the trailer's fold-down table.

"We got eggs," said Sayre, smiling at Ned. He was so clean.

"Smells great," he said politely.

Papa Gilles made Ned up a plate.

"So how is your pain?" asked Ned.

"I'm fine," said Papa Gilles, stretching and withdrawing his hands.

"All right. Well you know you don't have to suffer."

"I know."

People all over camp were hooked on Ned's drugs. He was good at his job. Lyra didn't mind him though. Ned had taught her to read.

"Where is the young lad?" asked Ned. He meant Brandon.

"He's getting older, you know, spending more time

doing his own thing," said Sayre.

"I see. Maybe one day he would consider Care Seminary. It's a good path, a righteous path."

"We would like that," said Sayre with a smile.

Lyra rolled her eyes.

Papa Gilles and Lyra set off on their journey a few days later. They had a few jars of beans, the cast iron skillet, and they took turns riding the bicycle. It was close to six hours to get there on foot. They planned to spend a few days, smoke a heap of fish, and then make their way home.

Lyra was in heaven. She felt safe with Papa Gilles walking beside the old highway. The sky was clear and the sun's warmth was like an embrace from above.

Going to White Mountain Forest would be the furthest that Lyra had ever travelled. It was the southernmost point of Coos County, or the 'Kingdom of Coos' as people in Dummer liked to call it. Since Lyra didn't go to school, that's what it was. The Kingdom of Coos stretched all the way from the City of Goreham to the north, Maidstone and Canaan in the west, the great Lake Umbagog in the east, down to Mt. Washington in White Mountain National Forest. This was her whole world. Although she knew that it was situated within the large and mysterious Land of New Hampshire, the most important part was Dummer Mobile Home Park in the heart of the kingdom. There were gated communities of rich folks up in Goreham she knew, but they had everything they needed right here in Dummer, so why leave? That was how she was raised, and she hadn't had occasion to question it yet.

As Lyra and Papa Gilles made their way past old farmsteads, some abandoned, some with gardens all around and chickens in the yard, she was amazed that they had never made this trip before.

"It's wonderful," said Lyra.

Papa Gilles just grinned. He was feeling it too. The sun on their faces, the rattle of the fishing rod bouncing around on the back of the bicycle, and the fresh air were intoxicating. Gilles was transported into childhood memories of life rambling out in the open, flushed cheeks, old friends long gone, and fish fried in butter and salt. He looked at Lyra.

"Glad yer enjoying it mousie."

He had intended to take the family down here long ago, but the years just seemed to slip away as day after day passed.

Well here we are, thought Papa Gilles.

After a few hours of traveling, there was an old well with a cast iron pump handle and a dirt path leading down to it. The house looked abandoned, but the pump looked well used.

Lyra and Gilles walked down to test it out.

"This was the old Patrie house," said Gilles. "We always stopped in here for a drink when we passed in the old days. Looks like they've moved on."

Lyra gave the pump a few cranks. It worked fine. They filled up their bottles. Lyra sprawled out on the grass, happily drinking the stone cool water in the warm afternoon. Papa Gilles hemmed and hawed in French, his joints popping and cracking as he got down slowly. He moaned in pain.

"You okay?"

"I'll survive."

They poked around in their bags and split a candy bar they were planning to save for when they got to White Mountain.

"We deserve it," said Gilles.

It tasted sweeter than anything Lyra had ever eaten.

They rested for a good hour.

"You'll have to carry me out of here my girl," said Papa Gilles finally. "My hips are locked."

Lyra put his arm over her small shoulders and did her best to help him up. She realized that there wouldn't be too many more years when he could make a trip like this on foot.

"I haven't walked this much in years," he said.

"Can you keep going?" asked Lyra, concerned.

"I'm not dead yet, calisse," he snapped.

"Sorry," she murmured.

They continued on their way.

All her life Lyra dreamed of one day living in White Mountain National Forest. In her mind it was like heaven on earth. She was almost afraid to see it in real life in case it didn't match her expectations.

Once when she was about seven and Brandon was a few years older, Papa Gilles and Sayre had taken them to Umbagog Lake with a few others from Dummer. They'd managed to get a ride for most of the way on a flatbed truck somehow, so they ended up driving for twenty minutes and walking for less than two hours. That trip had been difficult for Papa Gilles too, with his polio, but even then he didn't have the hooch gut he had now, and swimming in the waters of Umbagog Lake went a long way easing his joints.

The trip to Umbagog Lake was the best experience of Lyra's life. She remembered the magic of floating in deep waters, the light shimmering on the surface of the lake.

I could die happy now, she had thought, with her face to the sun. Lyra retreated into that memory often during unhappy times. It was at Umbagog that her love of nature was sparked.

This time it would be Lyra's first experience swimming in a river.

As the afternoon light deepened and expanded they grew closer to their destination.

"All the old things…" said Papa Gilles with emotion in his voice, his mind completely overtaken by memories.

Just before the town of Randolph, they exited the highway and journeyed down a dirt road.

"The house where I grew up is just up here," he said. "These roads were my highway when I was your age."

Finally they made it to the place they were looking for. The driveway was completely overgrown, almost to the point that it was unrecognizable, but there was the cabin, just like Papa Gilles had always said. It sat empty for decades now. Green moss crept up the walls, which were once red, but only the paint just below the roof remained. The steps were all rotted away but Gilles rolled an old washtub out from under the building and set it up as a step to access the door. It took some pushing and a good kick to get inside, but they did it.

"Calisse," whistled Papa Gilles.

Lyra looked around. It was dark inside, with no electricity and very small windows, but she was used to the darkness of the trailer. There was an ancient horsehair couch, a few beds with the bedding still on, all covered in dust, and a washup area with counters and old cabinets for storing food. She ventured in, poking through the cupboards. They were mostly bare. An old dresser contained threadbare clothes and some old toys made of metal and wood from a bygone era.

"What should we do first?" said Lyra. "Want to go fishing?"

Gilles sat down on the couch with a heavy and pained sigh. He was happy to rest.

"I need to sit for a day my girl. I'm not going anywhere. Maybe tomorrow…"

Lyra got to work shaking out the blankets in the evening sunshine. She remade the beds as best she could and gathered wood for a fire. It was getting late and her stomach was grumbling.

Gilles napped lightly, letting himself relax into old memories.

Lyra dug through the bag and pulled out their beans.

"Where are you going with that?" said Gilles sleepily.

"I made a fire pit," she said.

He laughed and sat up slowly.

"You don't need to cook outside," he said. "There's a fire cook stove right here."

He hauled himself up, rubbed his eyes, and went over to the enamel wood oven. He poked around inside.

"You'll have to check the stovepipe for animals and bird nests," he said. "It's probably full of them. But this here stove is solid as a rock."

There was an old ladder under the cabin. Gilles helped Lyra set it up alongside the house to clamour up onto the roof to check the stovepipe. Gilles was right, it was choked up with years of animal debris. It took Lyra over an hour to clear it out.

"That was my job, back in the day," cackled Gilles.

When Lyra got back inside, Gilles had laid out all his fishing tools.

He's excited, she thought.

Lyra was famished and filthy.

"If you go up in the bush thataways," said Gilles, "there's a brook where you can wash up."

Lyra picked her way through the forest in the direction Papa Gilles indicated until she found what he was talking about. There it was—the old brook. She washed her hands, her arms and her face and went back to the cabin. A trickle of smoke was puffing merrily out of the stovepipe. Lyra took a deep breath of fresh air and looked around her. It was both like and unlike how she imagined it would be. She turned in a full circle, enjoying the calming effect of being completely surrounded by trees with sunlight filtering through.

When Lyra returned inside, Papa Gilles had the beans in the cast iron pan cooking on the wood oven.

"Just wait til there's fish on this pan," he said. Lyra was looking forward to it, but for now the beans were enough.

Lyra pulled a dusty old box out of the back of the cupboard.

"What's this?" she asked.

Papa Gilles crowed with delight. It was an old box of tea.

"That's a hot drink, girlie!" he said, manoeuvring an old tin can onto the stove and filling it up with water from their bottles.

"It can't still be good…" said Lyra. "It's got to be what, forty years old??"

"I don't care, I'm drinking it," said Gilles.

They ate their meal together on enamelware plates and drank their tea from enameled tin cups when it was ready.

"Ain't too bad," said Gilles, sipping hot liquid.

Lyra thought it just tasted like dirty water but the warmth was soothing.

"There's wintergreen around here we can pick to make fresh tea," said Gilles. "I'll show you where to find it tomorrow."

Lyra was excited at the prospect of learning about the forest.

After dinner Lyra washed up at the brook, and by the time she got back, Papa Gilles was already asleep.

Lyra tucked herself into one of the other beds. The cabin was so dark she could barely see, and as the sun went down everything went black. It was like nothing she had ever experienced before because there was always some light or other in Dummer Mobile Home Park, from solar lights at least. She closed her eyes and let herself slip away into dreams.

When Lyra woke up, the morning was already late. It was the longest sleep she could remember. Her whole body felt rested. Her home was noisy and people were coming in and out of the trailer all night long. She had never had her own bed before either. Lyra lay there in the morning light, luxuriating in the comfort of being wrapped in blankets in her own bed. She sighed.

"Good morning, mousie," said Papa Gilles. He was likewise lying in his bed, curled up in the blanket, enjoying the peaceful morning.

"I'll go fill the water bottles," said Lyra, letting her feet poke out and onto the floor.

"Go explore," said Gilles. "Don't get lost though."

"You coming?"

"Crèche I ache all over… you go. Let me rest."

Lyra nodded and packed her bag for a hike. She set off in the direction of the brook.

Lyra stayed out all day. She started out on a mission to fill the bottles, but she ended up following the brook deep into the forest. At first she walked quickly, her head turning this way and that, her eyes greedily taking everything in. Eventually she slowed down, realizing the joy of taking in the little details of moss on fallen logs, tiny green leaves, thick trunks covered in corrugated bark, and the soft gentle song of cold water splashing over the rocks of the brook. When she slowed down, she saw so much more; she saw squirrels, so many different kinds of birds, insects, and the feces of different animals that she couldn't identify. She found good strong walking sticks for herself and for Papa Gilles. As she was walking she found many different shapes and colours of berries, but she did not recognize most of them to know whether or not they were safe to eat. She took note of their leaves and other details to tell Papa Gilles about later.

When Lyra returned to the cabin, Papa Gilles was sitting out front in a sunny patch like a cat.

"Hey," called Lyra. Her cheeks were flushed with life and her hair was wild. She was carrying two large sticks.

Papa Gilles laughed at the sight of her.

"This one's for you," she said, handing him the taller one.

She sat down on the ground beside the log he was seated on.

"I followed the brook," she said.

"Good girl. What did you find us for supper?"

"Nothing," she said, dismayed. "I don't know what to eat in the forest."

"This here land has everything we need. You know, this whole place was full of Abenaki living with the good earth before the white men built all those Megamarts. My gramma was Abenaki, lived to be a hundred."

Lyra was silent. She knew a little about that because of Joan Whiteduck.

"When we were kids, we grew a few things up by the cabin, but there was so much we got from these woods. Just cultivatin' the forest a little, a little tending here and there to keep the food things growing lush. It's not like Dummer where everything's picked bare."

"You'll have to show me," she said.

"Okay mousie," said Papa Gilles, but Lyra doubted it would happen. She had been asking for education all her life.

For supper they had more beans. Papa Gilles was still not up to the hike to the fishing hole.

"Tomorrow," he told Lyra. "I promise."

That night they went to bed, both dreaming of fish.

Lyra woke up the next day in a deeper calm than the morning before. She got up early and packed her bag for the trek.

"Ready?" said Papa Gilles. He was excited too.

They set out on foot back up the laneway to the main road, and then branched off at a different spot.

"Now it's been a really long time," he said. "Things could look the same or they could look a little different," he warned. He had noticed on the way up here that there were huge tracts of lands that were once forest but now contained falling apart houses or vast sand pits where over-eager developers stripped the land bare and then didn't have the capital to build the suburbs they imagined. That's why his mother had encouraged him to leave in the first place.

"No opportunities here," she had said. "When the forest is gone there will be nothing." He worked as a labourer with a crew of simple lads in Dummer, and before he knew it, they were all old men.

Finally they reached the spot. Lyra peered out into the water. She could see the bottom, and then the water was black with depth.

"That there's the fishing hole," said Gilles. "There's good trout down there."

He was turning over rocks in the damp moss around the trees at the river's edge.

"Haha," he chortled, pulling out worms and stuffing them in his shirt pocket.

Lyra dipped her toes in the water.

"Swim downstream," said Gilles. "So you don't scare the fish. And be careful!"

Lyra pulled off her jeans. She went to take off her shirt too, and hesitated. When she was a little girl at Umbagog Lake she just swam naked. Was she too old to swim naked now? All the grown women wore clothes in the water then. She frowned with uncertainty.

She looked at the water. She didn't want to wear clothes. She stripped off everything and jumped in.

"Caught one!" shouted Papa Gilles, beaming. "I still got it!"

He hooked the fish with a length of wire to his pants, letting it float captive at his side.

Lyra was careful to keep her footing. The river's current pulled at her like fingers, sometimes caressing her gently, but once in a while yanking her so that she was unsteady on her feet. It was difficult to swim here. It wasn't like floating in the still waters of Umbagog. The river had an active energy that Lyra could feel on every inch of her skin.

It was a perfect day. After over an hour in the water, Lyra came back up on shore. She squeezed out her hair and shook the droplets off her body. She got dressed. She was famished.

"Go make a fire," said Gilles. "Let's fry these up right here."

She peered in the water and saw that he had four fat fish on his wire.

"Those three are trout," he said. "See the markings there?"

Lyra looked closely and nodded.

"This other one's a big ole bass."

Lyra gathered a large bushel of sticks and bigger pieces of dry logwood for a fire. She noticed a perfect location on a large flat rock on the shore for a cook-spot. As she dropped the wood and hunkered down to build the cooking formation, she saw evidence of many fires before her. This was an ancient fishing hole.

She used her flint and steel on birch shreds to get the fire going, and blew it into life. It wasn't hard with the abundance of perfect sticks and a gentle breeze flowing down the river. In no time, she had a merry crackle going and her hair was almost dry. She tied it back in a short braid.

"The fire's going," she called out. She looked at Gilles. He had his special bone-handled knife out and was doing something with the fish.

"Hey!" she yelled, scampering over the rocks to where he was. She wanted to miss none of the teachings. She knew Papa Gilles would not repeat anything.

She watched closely as he bisected the fish up the stomach, scraping its guts into the river.

"Back to the waters," he said. Little fish swarmed over the guts, feasting. He removed the fins and popped out the eyeballs. One he tossed in the river. The other he saved on the rock.

'These here are a treat," he said. "We'll give one back to the fish and the river and the land, and keep the other for ourselves."
Lyra grimaced but said nothing. If Papa Gilles wanted her to try fish eyeballs, she would.

"Some people take off the skins, but they're damn fools," he said. "The skin's delicious. And it's good for you."

Lyra always ate fish with the skin on, but she remembered that it had a strong fishy flavour and some people, like Sayre, found it too much.

Gilles sawed off the heads and dropped them in the river.

"If we're hungry we eat these, but we'll be back tomorrow, so today we can give them back."

Gilles angled the cast iron pan onto the fire, letting it heat up to a suitable temperature. He could only fit two fish in the pan. The other fillets he laid out on the rocks.

"We shall feast, mousie."

The smell of the fish wafted out over the river. Water birds swooped close to investigate. Lyra's mouth watered.

The fish skins crackled and popped in the pan, providing oils for the meat to cook. Gilles rubbed his hands together. He was about to get a taste of his childhood.

Finally the fish was ready. Gilles dressed two clean sticks with several tasty morsels. He and Lyra gobbled them up. Lyra licked the juices from the stick, and Gilles refilled it. He laid the uncooked fillets into the pan.

"I'm glad it's not fished out," said Gilles. There were many spots in the area that were once filled with different kinds of fish, but swarms of people had either caught every last fish there was, or they poisoned the water with so much pollution that the fish that survived there were dangerous to eat. This particular water system was difficult to access because of the rocky mountainous terrain, so the ecosystem had largely remained intact.

Suddenly Lyra realized that they were being watched. As soon as the feeling prickled over her she noticed a man was standing silently at the forest edge of the path.

"Papa," she said.

He noted her tone and his gaze shot to the man.

"Kwai," he said.

The man watched them a moment longer, and then came forward.

"Kwai," he said back. He was holding a fishing rod. Papa Gilles relaxed.

"What did you say?" said Lyra quietly.

"It means hello," said Gilles.

They continued eating.

Gilles gestured to the man to join their meal.

"There's lots if you're hungry," he said.

The man smiled kindly and came to sit nearby. He pulled out a tobacco pouch and wooden pipe.

"What brought you to Manosek?" asked the man, packing his pipe.

"I grew up here."

"I see," said the man with surprise. He lit the pipe and took a puff. He passed it to Papa Gilles, who took it with gratitude.

"You speak the mother tongue," said the man, having a bite of fried fish and leaning back against the rocks comfortably.

"My grandmother taught me a few things," said Gilles.

"Welcome home," said the man. "I'm Soko."

"Gilles, and Lyra."

The man smiled at Lyra. He had kind eyes. His physique appeared younger from a distance, but up close Lyra could see he was probably Papa Gilles' age.

"Miigwetch for the fish," he said.

"May I try the pipe?" asked Lyra, looking at the man and sidelong at Papa Gilles.

He laughed until he coughed.

"Sure mousie."

Soko handed her the pipe and she took a tiny puff. Once Brandon had made her try a cigarette, and one puff made her spasm with coughing. This was cleaner, easier to smoke. It had a taste. She handed the pipe back.

"Thanks," she said.

"Miigwetch," he said.

"Meeg-wetch," she said, letting the word roll over her tongue.

They chatted with Soko for a while. He and Gilles fished some more while Lyra explored the shoreline.

When it was time to go, Soko gave Gilles a tie of tobacco.

"Safe travels, my friend."

"Miigwetch, you too."

Lyra and Gilles walked home.

They visited the fishing hole every day over the next few days and gorged themselves on as much fish as they could eat. Lyra's skin, hair and nails glowed from the fish oils. She had an incredible amount of energy. Papa Gilles explained that she had the life force of the fish inside her.

"That's why we give back to the river," he said. "To honour the life force." This was something his grandmother told him so long ago that he forgot it until he saw Lyra's inquisitive face.

They dug a huge pit in the ground and built up a large fire. Papa Gilles intended to smoke as much fish as they could carry back to Dummer. He was content to poke around and tend the fire all day while Lyra explored the bush.

"We should think about going back to Dummer," he said one day. "Sayre will be worried."

Lyra frowned. She knew they would have to return but she didn't want to. This was heaven on earth.

"Old Inas will be needing your help again too," he said.

Lyra looked at him sharply. He never let on he knew where she spent her days much before. Lyra thought of Inas and the plants. She wondered how they were looking.

"I guess going back's not so bad," she said. "But first teach me some more about the forest."

"I don't know what to teach you," he said. He always said that. It was frustrating.

"How about the tea?" she said. "Show me where to find it."

He took her out under the trees and showed her where to look around the trunks.

"Here it is, this plant here. You can make tea out of a lot of things, but this one here is what we used growing up."

He plucked a thick, waxy leaf and popped it in his mouth. He chewed, and then blew in Lyra's face. She could smell the minty, fruity oils in the leaf on his breath. She plucked one and munched. It was bitter, like the tea, but with layers of fresh-picked flavours.

"You can eat the berries, but don't go crazy on them," he said. "More than two or three will make you sick."

She picked one of the berries. It was pale green with a cloudy surface. It tasted much like the leaf, but a bit sweeter.

"Let's fry some up with the fish," she said.

Papa Gilles was taken aback.

"Well we could I suppose…" he said. "But we don't need to. Harvest some of that for tea, and I'll show you some greens that go great with the fish."

He took her to a patch of sunlight in the forest where leeks poked up cheerfully through the leafy mulch of the forest floor.

"Look at it in threes," he said. "Never take more than a third. So the forest can replenish itself."

Why didn't he show me this before? thought Lyra. *We could have been eating fish with greens all along.*

This was Papa Gilles' way. At least she was getting the teaching now.

She noticed another patch of sunny mulch. She ran over to it and identified the leeks.

"You got it, mousie."

Papa Gilles showed her all his favourite places to play when he was a kid. He even took her on a hike up to a waterfall in the forest. An ancient statue of a woman in a blue dress stood watch at the top. Lyra climbed up to her and explored her contours with her fingers.

"Joan," she murmured. It reminded her of Joan Whiteduck.

They traveled to a lookout point where the blue hills high above the river, beyond the forest in the distance, were surreal.

"Tomorrow we're going into town," said Gilles. "See if the Randolph General Store is still in business."

Lyra was both excited and filled with trepidation at the thought of seeing other people. Humans could be so awful, but sometimes there were special ones.

Like Basquiat, she thought.

Papa Gilles spent the morning catching a mess of fish, and they took off for the store.

The town of Randolph was small and clean. Some houses were falling into the ground, but it wasn't like Dummer, with piles of trash everywhere. Lyra remembered one of Joan Whiteduck's photos with a caption on it:

"We choose how we want to live."

She could really see that here, where even though the municipality had stopped collecting the trash, the residents had figured out another way to deal with it. She thought of the "leaders" of Dummer; there were really only Dougie Mustang and the Dummer Boyz. She snorted. No vision. No sense of community.

The town had a handful of houses built into the slope of a hill. Children were playing in the dirt road. Overall it seemed like a nice place.

Papa Gilles smiled. The old general store was still standing after all these years. Clusters of items hung from the rafters of the wide front porch, like rough-made pots and kettles, dried herbs and vegetables, long-wicked beeswax candles, and punch tin lights.

They went up to the front counter.

"You want to trade these fish?" said Gilles, waving his catch-wire filled with fresh meat.

"Certainly," said the young woman at the front counter, putting down the book she was reading.

Lyra inspected her with interest. The woman was wearing a homespun wool sweater over a loose-fitting linen dress. She smiled at Lyra.

"What are you reading?" asked Lyra.

"Peter Pan," she grinned.

"What's that?"

"Oh, it's a story about fairies and mermaids," said the woman with a laugh.

Gilles handed the fish over the counter. The woman weighed them in her hands and pulled out a long steel knife, much like the one Papa Gilles brought fishing with them.

"Sorry, I woulda gutted them but I didn't want them to go bad coming up here."

The woman nodded and lifted a fish to her nose and took a sniff.

"Still good," she said.

Gilles took out his knife and they gutted them together.

Lyra wandered around the store looking at all the things on offer. There were carved wooden bowls and other eating and cooking tools, and all sorts of things made of clay. Almost everything here was made by hand. The oil and gas prices had thrown the supply chain into chaos, so people who could make things were in high demand. In the big cities people used credits and money, but out here, handmade tools and skills were worth more than money. Sometimes Lyra dreamed about moving to the city when she was old enough, for the opportunity to learn new things and meet new people, but she didn't want to get trapped giving all her waking hours and energy and life force to some company job that told her what to do, what to wear, how to live. The capitalism trap. She heard about it from Joan's social media. At the same time, there had to be more to life than Dummer Mobile Home Park. She caressed the soft wood of the bowl.

Suddenly she felt eyes on her. She turned quickly and noticed the woman at the counter smiling at her.

"Did you make these?" asked Lyra quietly.

"No, that was Jeremy over in Errol. I'm the tinsmith."

Lyra looked up above her at the sparkling tin items hanging from the ceiling.

"You made all these?" she asked incredulously. "How?"

"With fire," grinned the woman.

Papa Gilles chose non-perishable foods in trade for the fish; salt, flour, and a bag of locally grown hops.

"For the lads at the Pickled Peach," he grinned. He had to pay his tab anyway.

He let Lyra pick one thing. She chose a brace of ten beeswax candles. They would last all winter lit sparingly on early nights and cold, dark mornings.

The woman at the counter eyed up the high pile of filleted fish wrapped in waxed paper. She reached over the counter and picked a small tin candle holder. It had a star pattern punched into the top. She handed it to Lyra.

"For your candles," she said with a wink.

Lyra curled her fingers around the precious shining tin.

"Thank you," she said with her serious expression.

Suddenly they heard a commotion of voices outside. Lyra tensed and prepared to hide. The woman looked at the door. Her expression was unsurprised and not alarmed. Lyra relaxed slightly.

"It's a rally," she said. "If you don't mind, I have to go." She got up from behind the counter and went to the shop door. Papa Gilles and Lyra followed. She closed the door behind them.

In the street out front of the General Store, risers were set up and there were some people who appeared to be preparing to speak. There was a small crowd of locals gathered. A man took to the stage. Papa Gilles and Lyra looked at one another. It was Soko, the man from the fishing hole. Beside him stood a young woman. She was hardly more than a teenager but she stood very tall and proud.

"It's… no it can't be…" whispered Lyra.

"Joan Whiteduck," said a man beside them. "That eco-activist."

"No she's a feminist," said another.

"No no, you'll see, she's an indigenous rights activist."

Post-capitalist, thought Lyra.

The man on stage turned on his megaphone. A woman with a camera began recording. A few people held up their devices to record video to post online, but there were only two or three. Lyra didn't bring her phone on the trip because it was irreplaceable, and it cost too much to charge very often; she saved it for her art posts online. Right now, she wished she had it.

Joan Whiteduck, she thought. *How is this possible?*

Soko began to speak. A teenager with a guitar and another with a clarinet began to play accompanying music.

"A hundred thousand years ago, speaking in your terms of time, our ancestors came here when this place was a tundra, with ice lakes."

Joan began to dance.

"Our roots grow deep in this land," said Soko.

Joan moved to the music with flourishing, confident gestures.

"Generation after generation have lived here through thousands of years of changes to the environment, the development of forests, the migration of vast herds of deer, through the ravages of destructive invaders…"
The music turned more dramatic.

"The Settlers' few hundred years of leadership have been a failure. It must be acknowledged. Our old ways have lasted thousands. It is time to reverse the insanity. I am not afraid. I carry hope. We will revive the good earth," he said with finality.

The musicians bowed to a smattering of applause from the young people in the audience.

"That's our Alex," someone said. One of the musicians was from this town. That's why Joan had stopped here.

Soko handed over the mic to Joan.

"Thank you Manosek," she said, addressing the gathered villagers. "I heard you eliminated plastics in your community so I had to come say hello."

"Who is she?" asked an old person. Some people were ecstatic, others were confused.

"I'm on my way to the White Mountain Free Zone," she said. "They're making magic there." There was more applause from the crowd.

"They've set up schools, and a medicine lodge, and they have reclaimed the old way of government," she said. "They are decolonized."

Lyra was in awe. Joan spoke each word with such conviction. It was incredible.

"I'm here to support the Abenaki protesters here in your town who are blocking the Goreham dam projects."

There were grumbles in the crowd. Some townsfolk did not approve of the youth traveling up to join the protests. It was dangerous and they were worried.

"If the project goes through, you will lose everything you have created here. Connecting those poisoned waters into your watershed will kill you. Fight the dam. Damn the dam!" she shouted, raising a fist. Many fists raised with hers.

"Listen to Soko and the Abenaki elders here who know how precious these waters are. They are not your enemies, good people of Manosek. They are knowledge-keepers. They love this land like you do and they want to protect it. Stand with them!"

The crowd cheered. Joan took a bow and handed off the megaphone. She descended from the risers.

"I heard your General Store no longer deals in

money," she said. Lyra could barely hear her over the commotion. "You trade and share here."

"I guess we do," muttered an old man, surprised that this practical economic development was something special to this young celebrity.

Joan pushed through the crowd to the General Store. She walked up the steps onto the wide front porch, just a metre or so from Lyra and Papa Gilles.

Lyra couldn't breathe. This moment was so surreal. She stared hard, taking in every detail. Joan talked like an adult but from up close Lyra could see that she truly was just at the cusp between adult and child herself.

I could reach out and touch her, she thought.

The shopkeeper opened the door and let just Joan Whiteduck inside. She locked it behind her.

"Well mousie," said Papa Gilles as the crowd started to disburse. "That was exciting. Time to head back?"

"Papa no! I want to see Joan again!"

Whoever that young lady is, I'm sure she wants to be left alone."

Lyra sighed. He was probably right. She followed him, pausing and looking sidelong at the General Store many times as they left.

On the walk back to the cabin, Lyra was chattier than usual. She explained to Papa Gilles who Joan Whiteduck was.

"She is basically the queen of the internet," said Lyra. "When she posts a call to action, everyone follows."

"What are you talking about?"

"Well not everyone… like, kids. Teens. You know."

"Hmm."

"She'll say something like 'don't go to school today', or 'everyone tie a ball of plastic bags on your City Council's front door', or 'deface capitalist propaganda', or 'reclaim the commons', or something like that. And millions of kids will do it."

The more she talked, the more Lyra wished she got the chance to talk to Joan.

What would I have said? she thought. She had no idea. But she still wished she had taken the chance. She felt like meeting Joan Whiteduck was a once-in-a-lifetime opportunity.

They got back to the cabin and got ready for bed. A million thoughts were running through Lyra's mind. She was filled with keen regret.

That night, Lyra couldn't sleep. She tossed and turned, unable to stop the thoughts springing up in her mind. *Maybe Joan stayed the night in Randolph,* she thought.

After more agonizing, Lyra decided to take a chance and go back to the General Store. *Maybe she'll take me with her, wherever she's going...*

The thought was at once terrifying and exhilarating. She had to take the chance. She slipped out of her bed and into the night as Papa Gilles snored in the bed nearby.

At first walking alone in the night air was thrilling, but soon Lyra was filled with doubts.

What if she's not there? What if she is? What will I say to her? What if something bad happens to me?

The darkness was heavy around her. The stars shed little light. Lyra felt like she had been walking for hours, and she hadn't seen the turnoff yet. She began to worry that she was lost.

Suddenly, she heard the faint sound of footprints on gravel. Someone was close by. She stopped dead in her tracks and listened hard.

Who else is out here walking at night? she thought.

She heard snuffling. It was an animal.

Lyra's mind raced. *What do I do?* she thought.

"Hello!" she shouted authoritatively. Most animals responded to a dominant voice by backing off.

She heard a deep-throated growl. It was very close. A chill ran up her spine.

I think it's a dog, she guessed.

"Hey there, it's okay," she said in a gentle but firm voice. She waited. The animal didn't move.

Lyra took a tentative step forward.

"I'm going now," she said. "I have somewhere to be."

She walked slowly at first, and then faster. The animal didn't growl, but Lyra could feel it following her. Her heart beat faster.

She started to run. Bad move. The animal barked and charged straight at her, pushing her dominantly with its huge head and grazing her leg with sharp teeth. It was a very large dog.

"Hey!" she shouted, slowing down. She reached down and touched her leg. The skin didn't feel broken but there would be a bruise.

"Bad dog!" she shouted.

She heard a little yip from further off. She squinted in the darkness but saw nothing. She had a feeling there were more out there.

Lyra felt a wave of fear. She realized now that this was a bad idea.

Should I turn back now? She wondered. *Or just keep going?* She took a few uncertain steps forward. The dog barked. She had a loud booming voice. Lyra shivered. She thought about Joan Whiteduck.

She's probably long gone, thought Lyra. *And I'm doing all this for nothing.*

She decided to go back to the cabin. She turned around and headed back the way she came.

By that time, the sky was beginning to lighten. The days were long and started early, and dawn was not far off. The dog was still following her. Lyra could see in the pale light that the dog was the biggest she'd ever seen. A tiny dog followed behind.

"Is that your baby?" said Lyra kindly.

The dog stared at her with unfriendly eyes.

"I'll leave him alone," she said. "Don't worry."

Lyra turned and ignored the little dog. She knew how dangerous bitches were protecting their babes. She kept walking.

"Go away!" she shouted, every once in a while. "Go home!"

The dogs followed Lyra all the way back to the cabin.

"You can't come in," she said quietly, trying not to wake up Gilles.

She slipped inside the door and went back to bed.

In the morning Lyra forgot all about the dogs. Papa Gilles and Lyra packed up their things and headed back to the fishing spot. The dogs were gone.

"I could live here forever," said Lyra happily, lying out on the flat rock in the bright summer sunshine at the fishing spot.

"We will be taking our leave soon," warned Papa Gilles. "Just enjoy the time you have."

Lyra intended to. She stripped down and waded out into the water.

"Be careful," called Papa Gilles.

Lyra was water-confident now. The river's pull was familiar. She crept out further, up to her shoulders. The current was strong and she clamped the rocky bottom with her feet. She closed her eyes and faced the warm sun.

Suddenly a mischievous water-finger pulled her sharply and her feet left the bottom. She scrambled to catch it again but her balance was thrown and the river zipped her out into the middle of the channel in seconds. Lyra was amazed how fast such a small river moved. A deep current pulled at her feet, plunging her underwater. She choked in a mouthful of river water. Papa Gilles looked up to see the sheer surprise on her face as the river spit her back up, coughing and slapping with her arms to stay afloat.

"Lyra!" he shouted, throwing down his fishing tackle and hobbling down the shore.

The current jerked her far out of reach, straight into a tumult of white water on rocks. She bashed against one large rock and then another. She was dazed with pain and

surprise, floundering uselessly against the power of the water. She rounded a bend in the river, unable to slow her course. Papa Gilles was long gone.
A large waterlogged tree that had recently fallen into the river loomed before her. She summoned her strength as she approached it and grabbed it with all her might. She thrust her body up and over the top, clutching the firm trunk with desperate gratitude. She coughed and coughed, sucking in huge gasps of fresh air. When she had caught her breath, she felt her whole body go limp with shock. She was utterly exhausted.

Lyra looked up and down the stream. There was no one around. The river flowed fast and steady beneath the branch, and Lyra realized that she wasn't safe yet. She would have to get from the branch to the shore.

Come on, she thought, gritting her teeth and willing her bravery to surface.

She took a deep breath and pushed herself down the log closer to shore. The tree wobbled wretchedly in the water. Her heart was racing and she felt panic well up inside her. She felt like she was going to pass out. She relaxed her body on the log and closed her eyes, willing herself to calm down. She was shaking.

Suddenly she heard a familiar bark. She looked up the branch, and there was the big black dog on the riverbank, shouting at her to get back on dry land.

"I know!" she shouted back. "It was stupid, I know!"

The dog continued to bark and bark. Lyra focused her attention on the sound, willing herself to stay conscious.

After what seemed like forever clinging to the log in the river with the dog yelling incessantly, she heard a human voice call out.

"Lyra!"

It was Papa Gilles.

"Lyra where are you?" he sounded scared as he approached the barking dog.

"I'm here!" she shouted. Then louder, "I'm here!"

He made a sound of relief, turning his head wildly looking for the source of the voice.

"Here Papa!"

His eyes locked onto the branch and he squinted. Recognition dawned on him and he walked faster.

"My mousie," he crooned.

When he reached the base of the tree, he tried to climb onto it, but he couldn't. His legs just couldn't bend like that, no matter how hard he tried.

"Damn polio," he cried. He reached out as far as he could.

The dog's barking subsided.

Lyra looked at the distance between herself and his hand. She felt a hot tear at the corner of her eye.

"You'll have to meet me halfway," he said.

"I can't," she said.

"You have to!"

"I can't fall in the river again," she said pitifully.

"Lyra, you'll have to grab my hand," said Papa Gilles. "I'm strong, you know that. Once I've got you I can pull you out. But you have to get here first." He reached out, wriggling his fingers at her.

She looked at his hand.

He's right, she thought. *There's no other way. I can climb to him or I can die here on this branch. No one is going to do this but me.*

Lyra summoned her will. She lifted herself up onto her knees and held the tree for dear life with her hands, shimmying down the branch. Her eyes blurred and she realized that she was crying.

That's it," said Papa Gilles. "That's it… you're almost there."

Lyra looked up and saw that it wasn't true, she had barely moved a few centimetres.

It doesn't matter, she thought to herself sternly. *All you can do is keep going.*

She continued her shuffle down the log sniffling piteously.

"Almost there, come on, almost there…" crooned Papa Gilles.

Lyra sobbed and climbed faster, scraping her legs on the bark. She clamoured over the last length quickly, practically jumping into Papa Gilles' arms.

"There there, mousie, brave girl," he said, holding her tight in his arms. "You're okay. Shhh, you're okay." He stroked her wet hair.

He let her cry it out. She felt him shaking too.

"You scared me half to death," he said with a laugh. "Mon Coeur!"

Lyra clung to him a little longer and then she stood up.

"Calisse!" he swore. She had bleeding lacerations all over her body, including a nasty purple area around the bottom of her ribs.

"It hurts," she confirmed.

The dog hovered just out of reach but close by.

"Who is this?" asked Papa Gilles. He reached out a hand in a cupped formation. The dog sniffed at his hand but didn't come closer. He noticed the elongated breasts.

"Where are your babies?" he asked. He scanned the bush and spotted movement. The dog's eyes tracked his. She growled under her breath.

"All right, all right," said Gilles. "Just calm yourself."

They made their way back along the shore. Lyra realized that she had floated a long way on the river.

I will not underestimate the power of rivers again, she thought.

The dogs followed along at a distance.

They found the fishing spot at long last.

Lyra groaned and bent down, picking up her clothes. She hurt all over.

"We could make camp here for the night," said Papa Gilles.

Lyra shook her head. She wanted to sleep in a warm bed tonight, even if it meant walking home battered and bruised.

Papa Gilles quickly gathered up the fishing things and they made the trek back to the cabin. He made a fire in the stove and tucked Lyra straight into bed.

"Rest is best," he said.

She fell asleep instantly.

CHAPTER 4: Joan

"Please be careful," said Joan's father before they ended their call. He was worried about her often, both because of her journey and because of her activism.

Joan Whiteduck's mother passed away two years ago. It was cancer. James, her father, was still fully heartbroken about it and had developed anxiety about Joan's safety. To be fair, Joan's journey presented risks on a regular basis. James knew that there was nothing he could say to change her mind though. She was like her mother in that way.

Joan was an eco-activist online for years, but her mother's death drove her to take her activism out into the world. She was travelling across Canada from her father's territory in Vancouver to bring her mother's remains back to her traditional territory on the east coast, with a few stops south of the Canada-USA border. The journey was an art installation processing grief for her mother, with stops along the way for eco-actions. Today she was marking a devastating oil spill by burning a large painting of the Earth weeping oil. Millions of youth around the world were doing the same in their communities. Next, she would visit a railroad blockade where a hundred youth were preventing logging trucks from accessing an old-growth forest slated to be clear-cutted.

Unfortunately world leaders had failed to address climate destruction. Too many of them were under the control of pollution-producing corporations. These youth, whose futures depended on preserving what was left of the wild ecosystems of Earth, had nothing to lose. In the last hundred years alone, more species had gone extinct than in the previous thousand, and such desperate times called for desperate measures. Even the little princes of the elites were joining the protests. Joan was the figurehead whose brazen actions emboldened her generation.

Joan's mother, Aniapsuin left a note for her daughter to read after her passing. The note explained that Joan's father James had another daughter from a previous relationship. They decided not to tell Joan, but Ania believed Joan should know now that she was losing her mother. One of Joan's reasons for returning to her mother's territory was to find her sister, who James believed was living out there.

"Don't you think it's a bit extreme to burn a painting?" asked a reporter.

"Burning the rainforest is extreme," said Joan, holding the painting high for the livestream. "Poisoning the water we drink is extreme. Killing every last bird, and tree, and animal to build petro cities is extreme. Ciy Planet is extreme."

"Yes, but what does this action hope to accomplish?"

"Children of Earth," said Joan, into the camera. "Do not participate in petro life. Oil and gas have messed up the world. No plastics, no petro. Do not participate. They need you, Children of Earth, to survive. Oil and gas end when you choose not to participate."

Cameras flashed. Joan held the burning painting stoically until it crumbled into ashes in her hands.

James was right to be afraid for Joan's safety. She received threats of violence, rape and death constantly. Joan brushed these off fairly casually with the boldness of youth, but Joan's life was in danger every day. For all the devoted followers she had, the Rage Machine complained about her every move, and there was an alarming number of grown alt-right men who took great pleasure in targeting and obsessing over a teen girl who cared about the environment. The government had not tried to stop her actions yet, but the logging blockade worried James. Burning a painting was one thing, but interfering with large businesses would definitely attract dangerous attention.

"Do you have to do it?"

"This is bigger than us already," she replied.

Joan knew that the men who hated these actions would probably eventually kill her, as they had many of the young women before her.

If the world is going to burn all up anyway, might as well die trying to stop it, she thought. She wasn't alone. Many of her followers felt the same way.

"Why are you doing this?" so many asked her.

"Eventually everyone who complains needs to realize that no one is going to do it for you; you have to do it yourself."

Joan was inspired to start the social account because of Allat. During the internet's early years people thought there would be an "Age of Information" where knowledge would be free and accessible through the power of wifi. Unfortunately the internet was flooded with an abundance of free fake information, and real research was password-protected. The free internet became simply corporate advertisement.

"Capitalist propaganda," Joan called it.

Joan had grown up in the post-Allat-era where

Joan's mother grew up in a town called Qonasqamkuk, "The Ancient Fireplace", a place colonials called St. Andrews, New Brunswick. Joan had visited only twice. She grew up her whole life with her father's people on the west coast. He was an accomplished engineer who had designed an important component of Valkyrie Snow's arcologies years before Joan was born. It was during his visits to the arcology building site for Mother House that he met Joan's mother. Joan was excited to visit these places as an adult and honour her mother.

CHAPTER 5: Lyra

Lyra spent the next day in bed. The bump on her ribs turned out to be pretty bad, and the bruise spread up and down her ribcage.

"Probably broke some of those," said Papa Gilles. "They'll heal up fine though. Just takes a while."

Lyra cuddled under the merciful comfort of the blankets and slept on and off, drinking fish broth occasionally.

"At least you've been eating well these last few days," said Papa Gilles. "That should help you heal."

Lyra's throat hurt from when she had choked on water. Her arms and legs were cut and bruised. Her ribs were definitely the worst.

Papa Gilles and Lyra spent a few extra days in Randolph. Not only was it good for Lyra to rest a bit more, but Gilles was afraid of what Lyra's mother Sayre would say about her injuries.

"Might as well stock up," he said, occupying himself furiously smoking as much fish as he could for the journey home.

Finally it was time to go. On their last night, Gilles fried up a pan of fish battered and seasoned with flour and salt. They went to bed with big round tummies. In the morning, Lyra filled their water bottles at the brook in the bush. As the crystal clear water gushed into the bottles, Lyra thought about what Joan had said at the rally.

If the dam projects go through, this water will be poisoned, she thought. *Why don't they listen to Joan?* Lyra figured that poisoning water that people were drinking was just about the worst crime she could think of.

She plucked some last greens to take back to Sayre and Brandon.

Brandon. Is he one of the Dummer Boyz now?

Lyra was startled by a sound in the bush. The dog burst out and came down to the brook to lap up some water. The puppy followed at his mother's heels, taking his cues from her and drinking beside her. He was very young, just fresh off the tit with floppy ears and bright eyes.

Lyra reached into her shirt pocket and pulled out some smoked fish. She held it out for sniffing, and then tossed it onto the shore. Her water bottles were full. She capped them and stood to leave. The dog accepted the smoked fish.

"Are we friends now?" asked Lyra. The dog came closer and bumped her leg with its big head and then jumped away.

As she walked back to the cabin, Lyra looked intently at the trees and rocks around her as though memorizing them. She would miss this place.

Papa Gilles loaded up the bicycle with their goods. The dogs scampered around the clearing.

"We can't keep them Lyra," he said. "We have enough to worry about." Sayre would not want dogs to feed.

Lyra ran her hand lightly along the dog's spine,

careful to avoid looking at the puppy.

"Hey what's this?" she remarked, feeling a strange lump. She looked closer and realized that both dogs had burn marks in their fur.

"They must have escaped a fire," said Papa Gilles.

The dog pushed its nose up to Lyra's side and sniffed her wounds. It licked her hand.

"Starlight," she said, remembering the diamond-encrusted starry sky the night she met the dogs. "Her name is Starlight."

"Don't you go naming them things," said Papa Gilles.

"I'll feed them," she said.

"Like hell you will." He continued packing.

It was early but the day was already hot. Mid-summer was upon them. Gilles closed up the cabin, and after one winsome moment with his hand on the doorknob, he and Lyra started the trek home to Dummer. The dogs sometimes ran off but they circled back every once in a while. Gilles said nothing.

At a crossroads on the highway, Lyra saw a poster on a fence. It was hand-painted and she was drawn to it instantly.

"White Mountain Free Zone," it said, with a map and instructions on how to get there. She turned to look at Papa Gilles. He could see in her eyes, plain as day, that she wanted to go there. His little mousie had a taste for adventure.

"You're still a little girl Lyra," he said. *Not for long,* he thought. "One day, you can follow the wind. For now, you're coming back to Dummer."

Lyra sighed and kept walking. She knew that someday she could choose which road to walk for herself.

They were back in Dummer Mobile Home Park that evening. Papa Gilles made a big deal of laying out their haul on the little table in the trailer to delay Sayre's reaction to Lyra's wounds.

"You were gone so long I was afraid you weren't coming back," said Sayre. "I was worried sick."

She smiled at the flour.

"It's been a long time since we had that," she said.

Lyra evaded Sayre for a few days and avoided the conversation about the river. She roamed the area, trying to occupy herself in the usual ways but she found that she was not satisfied. After seeing Joan in real life, she felt like she needed to be doing more. She longed to make art but she lacked the tools.

Lyra focused on helping Inas tend the vegetable beds, and on training Starlight and her puppy. Papa Gilles named him Grease Lightnin because he loved to run. Soon Lyra could pet both Starlight and Grease Lightnin. Her heart melted when she held Grease Lightnin in her arms. His little heart beating against his chest and his fresh smell filled her with joy.

One day while playing with the dogs, Starlight froze and the hair on her back prickled. Lyra looked around and realized that there was someone hiding behind a junk pile watching them. When he saw her look in his direction, he stood up. It was Brandon.

"Where did you get dogs?" he asked, walking toward them.

Lyra tensed up and Starlight took guard in front of her, baring her teeth.

Brandon slowed his approach, and then stopped completely at the menacing growl in the dog's throat.

"None of your business," said Lyra.

"Hey! Why are you being so mean to me?" he said.

Lyra frowned. "Go away," she said.

Brandon took a long look at the dogs.

"Fine," he said, walking off angrily.

That evening at the trailer, Sayre prepared a pan of mashed potato and flour pancakes for dinner for everyone. She was happy to see Brandon again.

"I heard you joined the Dummer Boyz," said Sayre with a laugh. "I knew it couldn't be true!"

Brandon frowned and shoveled pancake in his mouth. He had tried to join the Dummer Boyz, actually. They didn't want him because he was too young and scrawny and he didn't have a motorcycle. He wasn't worth the gasoline.

"You wouldn't be that stupid, would you," said Papa Gilles.

Brandon glowered and said nothing.

"Well I have news," said Sayre. She put her hand on her belly. "I think I'm pregnant."

"Calisse, Sayre," swore Papa Gilles.

"What? Aren't you happy for me?" she said indignantly.

"Sure, if the papa's a millionaire."

"Oh stop. It will be fun to have a baby again," she said.

Papa Gilles groaned, remembering how Lyra caterwauled all night as a baby.

"We'll be fine," said Sayre. She didn't mention that the father was long gone.

"How come Lyra gets to have two dogs?" said Brandon.

Lyra looked at him sharply.

"Shut up!" she said.

"Lyra that's not nice," said Sayre.

Brandon smirked.

"I want one," he said. "I want the puppy."

"No!" shouted Lyra. "No you can't!"

"Why not?" he asked. "Mum, can't I have one?"

Sayre looked back and forth at her children.

"Well it's only fair, Lyra," said Sayre.

Lyra looked at Papa Gilles. He looked away. He hated confrontation.

"The puppy is mine then," said Brandon.

"No," said Lyra softly.

"Don't be mean," said Sayre, losing patience. Maybe

if Brandon had a dog to occupy his time it would keep
him out of trouble.

Brandon grinned. Starlight was huge. Grease
Lightnin would grow into a monster.

Good luck trying to take him, thought Lyra. She
finished her pancakes and left the trailer. She had enough
of her family that day.

The following week the Dummer Boyz cruised into
the park for their next installment of "protection pay".

"Hey, whose dog is that?" asked one of the men on
motorcycles. They had spotted Starlight patrolling the
area around the park.

Brandon grinned wide.

"It's mine," he said.

"Hey it's the dopey kid," said another, coming closer
to admire Starlight, who had followed the motorcycles
into town with suspicion.

"She's vicious," said Brandon. "I could order her to
tear someone apart in seconds."

"Is that right?" asked one of the men.

"Quit talking bullshit," said the other.

Grease Lightnin marched up behind his mother. He
wagged his tail. By now he was letting strangers pet him.

"You got a puppy too?" said the first man.

Brandon's eyes sparkled at their attention.

"Yea," he said. "Just a sec."

He opened the door of the trailer and grabbed some
smoked fish. He beckoned Starlight inside.

"Come on girl," he said gently.

She stepped up into the doorway sniffing. She had
only been in the trailer a handful of times. She looked at
the smoked fish and trotted up to retrieve it. This was his
chance. Brandon jumped past her and slammed the door
shut with Starlight inside.

"I want to come with you," he said to the men. "I'll
bring my dog. Look how big and strong the mother is."

Starlight started to bark in the trailer. Her deep voice

was bone-chilling.

One man looked at the other. They were seriously considering it.

"What's stopping us from taking him right now and leaving your pansy ass here?"

"Dogs are a lot of work," he said. I'll feed him and take care of him and everything."

The first man laughed.

"Hey why not," he said. "Two pups to train."

Brandon scooped up Grease Lightnin in his arms. The puppy was not used to his touch and yelped. Starlight growled in the trailer and they heard her paws against the door. The whole trailer shook.

"Let's go," said Brandon.

"What about your other dog?"

"Don't worry about her, she's my sister's anyway. This guy'll be bigger than her in no time."

The men walked away and Brandon followed. Just like that he had joined the gang.

Lyra returned from Inas' house to find Starlight pacing around the camp frantically, darting back and forth, searching for her baby. She was making anxious noises and people in the park were nervous.

"Where is Grease Lightnin?" shouted Lyra, bursting into the trailer. There were deep scratches on the inside of the trailer door.

"I think the Dummer Boyz took him, Lyra," said Papa Gilles.

"What?! Where is Brandon?"

"I don't know," he lied.

"I know he had something to do with this," she said.

"It doesn't matter if he did. You have to let it go mousie."

"No! Poor Starlight!" The dog was howling outside.

"Shut up!" yelled a neighbour.

"I never should of let you bring those dogs home with us in the first place," he said.

Lyra stared at him dumbfounded. He wasn't going to do a thing about it. She was angry. She marched out of the trailer, slamming the door behind her. She hated Brandon, and right now she hated Papa Gilles.

"Starlight!" she called sharply. The dog followed.

Lyra went out to the place where she hid her bicycle. She was leaving. There was no way she was staying here a day longer. She pushed off and left the park with Starlight trotting behind her.

Where should I go? thought Lyra as she reached the highway. There was no way she could get the dog back from the Dummer Boyz herself. She looked at Starlight and felt a sharp dagger of guilt.

I'm sorry.

Basquiat. His name floated into her mind.

She decided to make her way to the Androscoggin Free Zone to see if it held what she was looking for.

Lyra took the familiar road. Maybe one day she would go the other way and visit Goreham, and see the skyscrapers, the gated communities of the rich surrounded by tent cities of those who weren't, the big hospital, and everything else she had only heard stories about her whole life. Today she was going to see Basquiat.

Lyra rolled up to the strip of old box stores. They were built in the last burst of economic development in the region back in the 1980s. They were not built well and several were falling into the ground. The General Store in Randolph, built a hundred years earlier in the 1880s with real stone and wood wrenched from the land, was built better and stronger than these giant box ghosts lining the highway. Still, Lyra could see that several of them were being actively worked on. She biked up to the one she had marked with her "Praise Jaune" piece. It was rough but she smiled at the sight of it. She longed to paint again.

"It's Joan Whiteduck," said a voice.

Lyra spun around to see a woman with long silver hair approaching. She wore loops of beaded necklaces and a dozen silver bracelets on one arm. Her hands were blotched with paint.

Lyra grinned. She was pleased as punch that someone else had seen and understood her art.

"Do you like art?" asked the woman.

"I do."

"Come over here."

The woman led her around the side of the building.

Lyra gasped. There was a massive mural in progress. She recognized the colour on the woman's hands in the bucket of paint sitting open on scaffolding. This woman was an artist.

"You're making this?" asked Lyra.

"I am. I would love some help, if you feel like it," laughed the woman.

Lyra's mouth dropped open involuntarily. She looked at the worksite, where a dozen buckets of paint sat amongst other precious art tools. She longed to touch them and inspect them closer.

"I would love to."

Lyra leaned her bicycle against the wall. She felt like this was a sign from the universe telling her she made the right decision coming here.

"I'm Glinda," said the woman.

"I'm Lyra Muse," she replied.

Glinda laughed, realizing that this girl was the author of the "Praise Jaune" piece.

"I am so pleased to meet you, Lyra Muse," she said. "Your work inspired me to create this mural, you know."

Lyra's eyes popped open with surprise.

"You never know who will be inspired by your art," said Glinda. "As artists we make things and put them out into the world, mostly never seeing the ripples created. I would love your help on this mural."

"This is Starlight," said Lyra, as the dog approached

and sniffed Glinda.

"Hello Starlight."

Glinda showed Lyra around the paints and different brushes and tools. Lyra lapped up everything with rapt attention. Glinda's mural was a bouquet of flowers in massive scale on the wall, and the colours were marked out in giant blocks with pencil.

Finally, it was time to put brush to wall. Lyra dipped a wide brush into a bucket of sumptuous dark green. She lifted it up to watch the thick liquid roll down back into the bucket off the end of the brush.

Glinda laughed.

"You love this!" she exclaimed.

"I haven't painted in so long."

"Creation sickness," she said, nodding knowingly.

Lyra looked at her with round inquisitive eyes.

"Creation sickness?"

"That's what I call it," said Glinda. "When I haven't made art in a long time and I'm filled with that longing to pick up a brush or a pencil."

Lyra nodded. She understood.

"I feel it so bad it hurts sometimes," said Glinda. "Creators have a purpose and a calling we must follow."

The two women spent the afternoon painting the wall. Glinda was thankful that Lyra didn't mind climbing up high on the scaffolding. She was grateful for the help.

"I've been asking Basquiat forever for an apprentice," said Glinda. "You've come at just the right time!"

"I know Basquiat," said Lyra. "I came here to see him actually."

"Let's take a break soon," said Glinda. "We can go have dinner and see him. I'm getting hungry."

Lyra was hungry too, but she had not brought a scrap of food with her. All she had was what was in her satchel and the clothes on her back.

Glinda showed her how to clean the brushes and store them properly.

"This is the boring part," she said.

"I love it all," said Lyra with genuine enthusiasm, eagerly taking in the knowledge.

"The best kind of apprentice!"

Lyra grabbed her bicycle and they went inside the building. Lyra stopped to take it all in. She wasn't sure what she was expecting, but this was like nothing she had ever seen before. The place was bustling with activity. To the left there were big pots of soup boiling steam and delicious aromatic spices into the air, and people rushing around pulling hot loaves of bread and other baked things from ovens. Makeshift countertops were lined with folks chopping up vegetables and fruit, and the clink of dishes and cups and cutlery filled Lyra's ears, along with the chatter of many conversations, singing, and laughter. There were long trestle tables getting set up for service right in the main area in the front of the building.

To the right was a jam space where people were playing guitars and sitting around on mismatched couches decorated with strings of twinkling lights. Lyra looked further. Holes were popped out of the walls lining the top of the building to let in light, and every window was different. Lyra noticed that there was a second level built up along the back inside of the building using a wide assortment of repurposed materials. Some of the upper level areas were enclosed, and others were left open to the main area. Hammocks hung there, and the upper floors appeared to be lined with blankets and pillows with an occasional bunk bed.

It was magnificent.

"Do all these people live here?" asked Lyra.

"We do. People have come from all around to build this Free Zone."

"Muse!" exclaimed a familiar voice.

Lyra turned to see Basquiat come toward them.

"I see you've met the Good Witch of the North," he said, looking pointedly at Lyra and Glinda's matching painted hands.

"My new apprentice!" said Glinda.

"I knew the right person would come along," grinned Basquiat. "Dinner's almost ready. Come sit."

He took them over to the table and sat down.

"So what do you think, Muse?"

"It's better than I thought," she said.

Basquiat and a few people close by laughed. Someone brought a basket of hot buns over and plopped it on the table in front of them.

"Go ahead," said Basquiat.

Lyra bit into the bun, feeling its warmth and simple dense flavour languish in her mouth a moment before chewing and swallowing.

Friendly people brought bowls of soup and plates of other snacks were passed around. Lyra could hardly believe this small beautiful world existed within the jurisdiction of the old one outside.

Free Zone. She could see what that meant more clearly than any adult.

After supper, everyone who didn't help with preparing the food cleaned up. As the evening progressed, people congregated in different areas, working on special projects, making music, or just sitting around socializing.

"You can bunk with me," said Glinda. "Come."

She led her new apprentice to a cozy nook in one of the upper chambers. Glinda had made a tent out of fabrics for privacy in a room with several others.

"Here are some blankets. You can sleep right beside me on the floor here if that's okay."

Lyra had never had her own space before anyway so it didn't bother her one bit. Glinda's nest was magical and full of interesting things. She fell asleep to a litany of not-unpleasant sounds of the night-oriented folks carrying on, under Glinda's twinkling lights and twirling blown glass crystals.

In the morning, Glinda took Lyra back out to work on the mural. There was much left to be done.

"Today we'll have to move the scaffolding," said Glinda. "Maybe we can get some help with that. Could be just us though!"

"Whatever you need."

"You look a bit young to be out on your own like this," said Glinda slowly. "If you don't mind me asking, how old are you?"

"I prefer not to say," said Lyra. The last thing she needed was to get kicked out of here because she was way younger than they all thought. She had heard Basquiat mention at dinner that the Androscoggin Free Zone was for ages seventeen and up. He had looked at her sidelong when he said it and she suspected he knew she wasn't seventeen. She was a tall string bean and her serious expression sometimes gave people the impression that she was older than she was, but seventeen was a stretch.

"I won't press." Glinda knew that Lyra might be leaving behind something worse than getting left out here on your own. Her own dad had been a miserable bastard. Best not to ask.

They worked side by side for hours in companionable silence. The time flew by. Glinda would occasionally give Lyra corrections in a gentle but matter-of-fact way. They covered twice the real estate on the wall, and by the afternoon Glinda was tired. She sat down and pressed her lower back with her knuckles, massaging out the kinks. For the first time, Lyra noticed that the artist was an elder. Her unusually bright spirit made her seem much younger than she was.

"Let me get you something to drink," said Lyra. She fell naturally into a care role the way she did with Inas or Papa Gilles.

"Thank you dear."

Lyra fetched water and they sat in the blazing sun, surveying their work.

"Let's go in for a siesta," said Glinda. "We can come back to it tomorrow."

Lyra could have painted all day, but the sun was quite hot, and she noticed when she got the water that the compound was actually quieter during the afternoon than it had been at night.

The two women went inside. The air circulated quite nicely with several very large fans on the ceiling so it was much nicer in here than the afternoon heat out on the asphalt. They washed their hands and faces and then went up to Glinda's nest for a nap.

After a few hours, Lyra woke up. Glinda was still sleeping beside her. She got up quietly, careful not to disturb Glinda's rest, and crept downstairs.

Lyra had not yet explored the entire back annex of the old Megamart building. Several areas were separated with old store walls rearranged, as well as new walls constructed from recycled materials. There was a carpentry shop, various artisan workspaces, and even a welding bay at the back. As she circled around, her breath caught in her throat. Just behind the open space with the couches, there was a community library. She walked quickly to the shelves, eyeing the books hungrily, scanning titles for anything to do with art.

"The Art of Architecture," she read. *By Valkyrie Snow.* She slid the book off the shelf. She flipped open the About the Author flap. "Cape Breton Island, Nova Scotia, Canada" she read to herself. *Canada, where Joan Whiteduck is from,* she thought.

She looked around. Could she just take the book? She looked over at the couches. If she sat there she could ask the next person using the library what the process was.

She settled into a cozy spot with the most light and opened the book.

Lyra found that she had difficulty understanding all of the words in the book. It was a derivative of Valkyrie Snow's PhD dissertation, after all. She pulled her device out of her satchel to look something up. It was long dead.

"Do you need to charge that?" asked a young woman approaching the couch with a book.

"Oh. Yes it's dead."

"Right over there," said the woman. "There's a charging brick. Just unplug one that's charged."

Lyra scurried over to a mass of cords on a power bar. She found a device at 100% and plugged her own in its place. She felt odd leaving it there. The old phone was one of her most prized possessions. It looked like everyone around here trusted each other though. She went back to the couch, and oriented herself so that she could keep an eye on it.

"Thanks," she said to the young woman. It was kind of them to let her charge it.

"We have solar panels and wind turbines on the roof," said the woman. "Ever since we hooked those up, life's been pretty luxurious around here." She laughed.

"Hey, can I ask you something? How do I borrow books from the library?"

"Just like this," said the woman. "No one will take the books too far. If anything gets to be a problem here, we revisit it in our monthly meeting. So far it's been fine."

Lyra nodded and opened the book back up. When her phone was charged she would look up the hard words. For now, she took in what she could and closely inspected the detailed drawings in the book. Lyra enjoyed the order and balance of meticulous lines drawn with a ruler and razor sharp pencil.

By dinner time Lyra's phone was charged. She scrolled through her accounts. The internet was painfully slow because there were so many people sharing the pirated network. She was now logged into the Free Zone's fast private internal server as well, where she had access to a huge resource of films, audiobooks, and other shared media.

"Hey, check this out," said Basquiat. He pulled out

his device and showed her a photo of her Jaune piece on the Androscoggin Free Zone's social media account. Lyra scanned it with interest. Her eyes smiled.

"Cool," she said.

"Wait for it," he said, scrolling down. It had thousands of 'Likes', and there were a multitude of comments. He stopped at one in particular.

Boom I love this, it said.

It was Joan Whiteduck herself. This time Lyra actually smiled.

"Is that seriously her?" she asked incredulously.

"It's her, Muse," he laughed. "She likes your shit. Excuse me, your stuff."

Lyra sat back and took it in.

Joan Whiteduck has seen my art, she thought. *Joan Whiteduck likes my art.*

People passed their empty plates to the end of the table to be collected by the washers. Lyra scraped any remains of dinner on plates onto hers. Starlight seemed to be able to find food on her own, but Lyra worried that she might go wild if she didn't make it worth her while to stick around here.

Just as people started to leave the table, the door opened and a stranger appeared. A few people looked over with curiosity. Lyra followed their gaze to the door. It was a woman, not old, not young, dressed for travel with a large rucksack that looked rigged for camping.

"Hello?" she said.

Basquiat jumped up.

"Hello there," he said with warmth in his voice.

As he approached, the woman filmed him with a small, inconspicuous camera.

"Hi," she said, holding out her hand to shake his, "I hope you don't mind." She wiggled the camera in the air with the other hand. "I'm a filmmaker. My name's Sikivu."

Basquiat reached out and took her hand.

"I don't mind at all," he said.

Lyra saw something in his smile that she had never seen before. She slid out from the table with her plate of scraps and went outside.

"Starlight!" she called. "Starlight!"

Eventually the dog came to Lyra. They lay down together on the cement. Lyra fed Starlight the scraps and scratched her belly. The nursing breasts had almost completely shrunk back down to size.

"Poor baby," said Lyra. She resolved to sneak Starlight up into bed with her later if the dog would permit it.

When Lyra went back inside, laughing people were scrubbing the dishes. The tables were put away. It appeared that a band was setting up.

"It's dance night," said Glinda, resting an arm lightly on Lyra's shoulders.

Lyra gazed around the room and her eyes landed on someone hanging a disco ball from a cord from the ceiling.

Is this place special, or is it just how the world should be? she thought.

She saw Basquiat sitting with the filmmaker over on the couches. She scooted over.

"Sure, the government is leaving us alone now," Basquiat was saying, "but right now we're not 'productive', not to any great extent… once we have more gardens and animals, and any reserves, there will be something to exploit."

"So you're an anarchist then?" said the woman. She was filming him, obviously, but the camera was set up on the top of the couch quite inconspicuously.

"Anarchist? I don't know… all I know is I see Banger Jones more than I see my state representative."

"Banger Jones? That's the gang leader around here right? For the Fraternity?"

"The Fraternity is for elites. Big city mob bosses serving billionaires. These country Proud Boys are just flunkies."

"So you like the gang system that's spreading across the rural areas?"

"No. We are responding to the gang system. Because some city slicker in the White House never will."

"I see."

"Banger Jones and all them, they are survivors, like us. Survivors of capitalism. We're all finding a new way. Those guys, they're using exploitation, fear, force. The tools of the old way, of capitalism. We are building something out of love."

"And this compound, how does it run?" she asked.

"It's an arcology," said Lyra quietly.

They both looked at her.

"I read about it today," she said. "It's a single building that serves a whole community's needs."

"That's right," said Basquiat.

"Does it serve everyone's needs?" asked Sikivu.

"Food, music, art… what more could you want?" Basquiat smiled wide and leaned back in the cushions. "And usually it's seventeen-plus around here, but Muse managed to sneak in somehow."

"So no families?" asked Sikivu. "Then how will the community be sustainable?"

"We're not ready for that," he said uncomfortably. "One day, but not yet."

Lyra left the adults to their conversation.

Soon, it was time for 'dance night'. Just about everyone came onto the dance floor at some point. The band improvised steady beats for movement and Lyra was fascinated. She had never seen live music with so many instruments before. There were guitars in Dummer Mobile Home Park, but that was about it. She had seen concerts online but they were so heavily produced that they might have taken place on an alien planet. This was a raw magical experience, being moved by music co-created by these beings in flow together. She realized that musicians were artists like she was. They probably got Creation Sickness too, like she did. She honoured them with some dancing, and then as people started passing around marijuana, and bumping and grinding, she decided it was time for bed. As she slipped away she noticed Basquiat and Sikivu dancing close.

Over the next few days Sikivu went to the various groups within the Androscoggin Free Zone community and interviewed people of interest. She was a documentary filmmaker and she was working on a project on the Free Zones. She had travelled up to Canada and made a fairly famous piece about the Cape Breton arcology community Lyra had just read about in the Valkyrie Snow book, *The Art of Architecture*, to Lyra's bemusement. Sikivu was less interested in the art and architecture of the place, and more interested in neo-governance. Doing that documentary sparked her interest in the growing Free Zone movement down south in her own country. She enjoyed travelling to other countries to see where the paradigm was shifting, and she was also keen to document it in her own culture. The Androscoggin Free Zone was a great example. What kinds of micro-governments were emerging as larger governments scaled back?

Sikivu wanted to continue making films abroad for a few years but she worried that too much time spent away and she would not be able to return. The USA borders were unstable. Several major real estate pieces had seceded from the union of states, like Pacifica (formerly California). Texaca, which was once Quiche and Aztec territory, then part of the state of Mexico, then united in the American Union, was now an autonomous nation-state. Many other states and regions had declared themselves autonomous as well, but with each election, regardless of the outcome, American presidents were focused on squashing the small secession movements, and that included further militarization of borders.

The USA became the de facto most powerful country

in the world after World War Two left colonial Europe decimated, by virtue of profiteering and playing both sides. In the decades after the war, countries around the world developed sustainable governments funded largely by taxation and public resource management with the goal of creating a middle class, a stable social system and resulting stable economy. USA peaked in the 1970s, but American policies fell short of the "first-world" model being developed elsewhere, and America never built a national education system, public healthcare, and many public works were divested to private enterprise. A very similar situation occurred in Turkey, when the government began to sell off public works. It created an artificially inflated economy for the short term, but by the turn of the millennium, both Turkey and the USA were experiencing third world living conditions for the non-elites. Instead of good leaders training and rising within a large, well-funded government with a large candidate pool during election time, unqualified figureheads backed by corporate interests would form a regime, win the election through populism, use the position to funnel money into their businesses, and then eventually be toppled by a new regime. Well-meaning politicians were either killed off, squeezed out, or simply could not garner the support of the masses, who had no loyalty to a federal government that was so small and provided no services, just a military and a nationalist agenda. By the 2000s, any kind of social service was defunded to pay for a series of oil wars in the Middle East, and by the 2040s, expensive walls were constructed around America's borders, half to support the nationalist agenda and half to embezzle money into the regime of the day's construction enterprises.

The secession movements were local governments and powerful organizations that wanted out of the corrupt union.

The "Free Zones" were more like libertarian commune micro-utopias. Their internal cultures varied region to region, but generally, if they self-identified with the Free Zone movement, they were focused on preserving what they perceived to be the positive values of their local culture, which were being eroded by an inadequately social central government. The key was to develop peaceful mutual aid networks amongst other Free Zones, and to stay small and downplay any military connotations. During the Pacifica Uprising, there was a mass purging of the "Pacifica Free Zone" because they had an armed militia dressed in fatigues. Colonial America had always been a war zone, from the bloody civil war that "united" the states, to police killing BIPOC and white citizens carrying guns, but for a time, during America's peak, the wars were fought on foreign soil. The warmongering culture of the colonials turned on itself in the end, and the American branch of the old British Empire was murdering its own independence.

Sikivu had a better understanding of the USA situation because of her time spent abroad.

"It's bad everywhere… this is the greatest country in the world," the news and the regimes had proclaimed when she was growing up. After visiting many other countries, she knew that wasn't true. When she started making documentaries, she was uninterested in politics and she had no interest in challenging the status quo. She just wanted to tell stories with film. However, after the success of some of her projects, she realized that simply telling stories with real footage and real people was a political act. Every piece of art she made was taking her deeper into dangerous territory. Admittedly, she liked the fame, and of course she needed the money, but she worried that eventually her ambition would kill her, because nothing was going to stop her from making films.

Sikivu asked Glinda for an interview.

"Sure," said Glinda, finishing the spot on the mural that she was working on. Lyra continued painting. "What do you want to know?"

"Tell me about how you got here, for starters. Then

I'd like to know about your artistic practice."

Glinda shared a little about herself. Lyra was surprised to hear that Glinda had children, long ago.

When Sikivu was done the interview, she turned to Lyra.

"Bas told me that you did that piece on the other wall and Joan Whiteduck liked it. That's interesting." She turned the camera ever so subtly onto her new subject.

She's good at that, thought Lyra.

"Yea she saw it, online."

"That's pretty amazing for a kid," said Sikivu. "Was that your goal?"

Lyra shook her head and considered why she did it. "The idea for it popped into my head and I thought about it all the time until I could make it."

Sikivu zoomed in on Lyra's face, getting the detail of her gentle features and her wide, serious eyes.

"Did you go to school?" asked Lyra. "You're smart."

"I did, for journalism. Where do you go to school?" asked Sikivu.

"Nowhere," said Lyra.

Sikivu frowned and the camera wandered. "I don't think kids should be here without access to education…"

"Never have. And I just got here. And there's more books here than anywhere I've ever been."

Sikivu was silent. She grew up in a fairly wealthy family in a gated community with its own academy and she had no direct experience with public education.

Surely there's some sort of schooling in every community, she thought.

The delusions of the wealthy had to be peeled back like an onion. The trouble with making them see was that they didn't want to see, because cheap clothes from China were convenient, nevermind child labour and destroying local economies, and gasoline vehicles were popular, nevermind tar sands and climate destruction.

"Did you run away from school?" she asked, directing the camera right at Lyra. "You didn't like it?"

"Only rich kids go to school."

Although Sikivu didn't totally believe that could be true, she felt a chill of truth run up her spine. She shook it off and continued filming.

"Joan saw your artwork through the social media account of Androscoggin Free Zone. Do you have your own channel where you promote your work?"

"No," said Lyra. "Well yes I have an account for Muse. It's private."

"You could make a career out of your art if you promote it online and monetize it."

"It's not good enough for that," said Lyra quietly.

"It's not good enough? But this piece is great."

"Well it's good enough for me," said Lyra. "I'm happy with it. But I don't need to share it. It's not really something people want to see." She looked sidelong at Glinda, painting the wall. "I'm going to get back to painting now," she said.

"Okay." Sikivu walked along the wall, gathering pickups of the women painting.

After Sikivu left, Glinda turned to Lyra.

"It's okay to be private with your art," she said, "as long as it's because it's what you want, not because you don't think it's good enough to share."

Lyra was silent.

"We all go through this honey," she continued. "At some point, you realize that your art's value is not in what it looks like. There is no such thing as good enough or not good enough. It's about how it makes people feel, including you. You are an Artist. You have the gift. You owe it to the world to share that gift. You don't know who needs to see your art. It could be a million people, like Joan's art, or it could be just one; we don't know the Universe's plan. But don't just keep it for yourself. Share it with the rest of us, please." Glinda smiled.

Lyra considered that as she painted the wall.

Yes, she thought. *One day I'll share my artwork publicly. But I think I could spend so much time trying to*

*make "Likes" and money that I wouldn't make art. That's
something I need to figure out first.*

Over the next few weeks, Glinda gave Lyra some
lessons on brush techniques, blending, types of paint, and
tips for linework. She even taught Lyra how to make her
own small fine brushes for detail work.

"I just clip hanks for bristles from my own hair,"
said Glinda. "But you could make some interesting
brushes with Starlight's hair, I bet," she said. "Bas keeps
promising to get us horses here to ride, and we'll be able
to make big brushes then."

Lyra thought about how long it would take to get
horses.

Will I still be here? she wondered. She had hardly
thought about home at all, but she knew she would have
to return there eventually.

She clamped a strip of copper hard with a wrench
to hold the bristles in place around the brush she was
making. She held up the brush triumphantly.

"You got it!" said Glinda. "Now all you have to do is
trim it to size."

Lyra picked up the scissors and did as she was told.

It's perfect, she thought, twirling it in front of her
eyes and admiring her handiwork.

"Thank you," she said, very serious.

Glinda reached over and squeezed her hand gently.

"You're welcome, my apprentice."

Lyra became obsessed with making brushes. She
constructed a range of sizes and shapes, cutting off most
of her hair at odd hanks and angles. She made friends
with the couple in the fabric workshop in the Free Zone,
who helped her transform old scraps of denim into a
carrying case for her art tools. She carried it around
with her everywhere in her satchel. Glinda's paints were
heavy-bodied gallon buckets from old construction sites,
but she told Lyra that more subtle paints could be made
from the honey and wax of bees mixed with pigments.

That kind of paint she would have to use on paper.

"Where do we get that?" asked Lyra.

"We'll have to make it," said Glinda. "It's not that hard, with old newsprint."

Lyra and Glinda spent a day making paper using old window screens pulled out of abandoned buildings. They spread their paper out to dry in the sun on the Free Zone trestle tables.

"See how they're gray from the newsprint ink?" said Glinda. "They'll have to be primed with a white wash before we use them."

Lyra was gobbling up all the knowledge she could, and the joy of intergenerational mentorship was inspiring Glinda in her own arts practice.

By this time, days had turned into weeks and the artists were putting the finishing touches on Glinda's mural. Finally it was complete. They stood back to take in the full finished picture.

"It is everything I imagined it would be," said Glinda. "Thank you for your help."

The corners of Lyra's lips turned up into a rare smile.

They stood enjoying their work for a few minutes. Lyra heard someone talking around the corner. It was an unfamiliar man's voice, and he was grumbling. She looked at Glinda and then walked to the corner of the wall. She peered around to see who it was.

Around the corner a man in filthy overalls she had never met before was standing beside a delivery truck smoking a cigarette. He was looking up at the "Praise Jaune" tag, muttering to himself, it seemed.

He noticed her approach.

"Joan of Arc," he said. Lyra could tell by his tone that he meant it as a bad thing.

"I like that," said Lyra softly, filing it away for a potential remix on this piece. "I might use it."

That was not the reaction the man was looking for.

"You're the one that drew that Squ*w Princess, did you," he said, spitting on the ground.

"We don't talk like that around here," said Basquiat, coming toward them.

"Brainwashed Commies!" shouted the man. He was suddenly angry.

"No need to get upset," said Basquiat calmly.

The man was furious for some reason.

Maybe he's dangerous, thought Lyra. There were a few people like that in Dummer Mobile Home Park, on the edge of keeping it together. Mostly they weren't dangerous. But they weren't driving trucks either. Vulnerable people were targeted and radicalized by bot accounts sponsored by companies intent on interfering in American political stability, pushing simpletons to divisive extremes.

The angry man shouted a racial obscenity.

Basquiat took a step forward, positioning himself slightly in front of Lyra and Glinda, but said nothing.

"I see you're taking children into your sex cult now," said the man, eying Lyra lewdly. "Pedophiles! I knew it!"

"Go on now, get gone," said Basquiat. "I was going to invite you in for lunch, but your vibes are bad, man. We can't have that in here."

Several other people came out of the arcology to see what was going on.

The strange man laughed and dropped his cigarette butt on the ground. He hawked up and spit once more, and then walked off.

"Sometimes things are ugly in this world," said Glinda quietly to Lyra. "All we can do is keep making art."

Lyra nodded absently. She was already thinking about her next piece, "Jaune of Arc".

They all went inside to get lunch. The tables were out in the old parking lot with drying homemade paper on them, so everyone took their lunches to eat on blankets on the ground outside, like a giant picnic.

"Like old times," someone said. This was how they

ate before they built the trestle tables. Lyra was reminded that they built this place from just an empty shell of a Megamart into the arcology it was.

Lyra looked out at the gardens they were building beside the highway. *I bet when these box stores were built they could not have imagined that this would be the future,* she thought.

She tried to imagine the lifestyle that supported the box stores. As a child who had never witnessed the cars that used to fill this highway or these vast stretches of cracked asphalt parking lot, it was difficult. Disruptions to the supply chain combined with economic downturn and an unstable supply of oil and gas made this strip of commercial buildings beside the highway inaccessible and impractical to many of the people who once shopped here. When the stores closed, one by one, the area became a food desert, which meant that there was no accessible place to buy food nearby, so the area depopulated. The people in the Androscoggin Free Zone reclaimed this land where no one lived any longer and they were learning to grow what they needed themselves, like the people thousands of years before the box stores were built.

Lyra wondered where Basquiat would put the horses. She looked down the strip and realized that there were enough empty buildings to house lots of different animals. She remembered Bas' comment to Sikivu, that it was only a matter of time before the Free Zone was noticed and exploited for what they had built here. Lyra thought of the Dummer Boyz slapping Dougie Mustang in his fat stomach. She shuddered. They would not leave the Free Zone alone, she realized.

CHAPTER 6: Lyra

Lyra spent her days reading books from the library and practicing her painting skills. Her hand vibrated with pride as she used her homemade brushes and paper. She was deeply grateful for Glinda. Teachers were precious, and she'd had so few in her life. Her birthday came and went with little celebration. She was thirteen now. Even though she was a teenager, occasionally she was reminded that the Androscoggin Free Zone was an adult community and she would have to leave eventually.

Basquiat was a compelling leader because his personality was wonderfully magnetic, but he didn't have much leadership experience so some things took a long time to get done. For example, the garden project should have long been completed by now, but since most of the community stayed up late, by the time everyone got up it was well into the afternoon and the sun was too intense for labouring too long outside. It would be another lean winter when they could have had a lot more than potatoes and corn stored away. Unfortunately for Basquiat, no one else had really come forward in leadership and it all fell on him to take it upon his shoulders.

The commune started with just a group of friends living intentionally, but now that there were elders like Glinda among them to care for, there was pressure to be a bit more organized. Still, things were progressing nicely, and when Lyra heard people complaining about things at Androscoggin Free Zone community meetings, sometimes she wanted to laugh when she thought of how things were organized at Dummer Mobile Home Park. The heat of summer deepened and ripened to perfection. Lyra took long walks around the area with Starlight following a few paces behind her or running ahead to scout. She gathered different leaves, berries, mushrooms, and flowers to bring back to Glinda for making into paints. She felt blissfully free. Sometimes she would scavenge through abandoned houses and find strange treasures of past lives.

"Be careful," Glinda warned her. "You never know what, or who, you could find in a house that looks abandoned."

One day she was rooting through an old clothing store, looking for shoes that would fit her. She had stretched up a few inches in the last few months and her shoes were too small. She would need to find a winter coat too.

"Aha!" she exclaimed, pulling a jacket with fringe on the arms out of the stock room. She put on the coat and checked herself out in a full length mirror. Her eyebrows rose in surprise; she looked years older in the small adult jacket. It was a bit wide in the shoulders, but overall a pretty good fit.

Lucky find, she thought, twirling around and letting the fringe fan out around her.

Suddenly, she heard a noise. She spun around to see a man entering the store. She froze, hoping he wouldn't see her.

No such luck. His eyes landed on her, and he smiled.

It wasn't a friendly smile.

She cast her eyes in both directions, looking for a way to escape. The only way out was through the front door. She was trapped.

"Hi girly," he said, taking a step in her direction.

Lyra was tongue-tied. What should she do?

The man took a few steps closer.

"Please go away," said Lyra. She didn't know what else to say.

"Don't be scared," he said. He spread out his arms and Lyra felt like he would grab her if she tried to run by him.

"Don't come near me then," she said.

The man walked even closer. Now there was just an empty clothes rack between them. Lyra looked left and right. The man's eyes followed her gaze. He grinned at her.

"There ain't nothing to be scared of," he said.

Lyra took a chance and dodged left. The man lunged left and grabbed at her, narrowly missing her sleeve. She ran down the empty rack and he doubled back to the front door. Lyra reached it first and burst outside with the man so close behind her she could hear his heavy breathing. His arm snapped out and grabbed her by the hair, entwining his fingers right up to her scalp.

Lyra let out a piercing scream. She was just outside the door and he was trying to pull her back inside the shop. She yanked and felt strands of her hair rip into his hands, but he had such a handful that there was no way she would be able to pull herself free. She slammed her body as hard as she could against the door, squeezing his arm.

"You little bitch," he growled, getting angry. "Why are you running from me? I'm not going to hurt you!"

"Starlight!" she hollered at the top of her lungs. "Starlight!"

From around the back of the building, Starlight came running. She let out a beastly cacophony of barks in her deep voice.

The man was startled and loosened his grip for a moment. Lyra yanked free with a scream and fell forward onto the pavement, catching herself with the palms of her hands. She scrambled to her feet as Starlight jumped up onto the door of the store, snarling and showing her massive teeth as her saliva sprayed the window. The man on the other side of the glass backed away a few steps. Lyra whirled around.

"If you follow us I'll feed you to my dog," she yelled.

"Jeez, fine, it was just a joke," said the man through the glass, backing away into the shadows.

Lyra frowned and prowled away from the store slowly, keeping an eye on the exit. Starlight continued barking, ready to do serious damage if necessary.

What if he has friends? thought Lyra, scanning the area for signs of more men. She realized that she was shaking. Her palms were bloody and full of little stones where she fell, and her head was throbbing.

"Starlight!" she called. She didn't want the dog out of her sight. "Starlight!"

The dog came trotting over to her. Lyra got down on her knees and hugged Starlight close with a sob. Then she got up, wiped away her tears, and walked back to the Androscoggin Free Zone with Starlight beside her.

Back at the arcology, a few people were gathered around watching a video on a phone. There was a sickness going around. The regime denounced it as a hoax, but the hospitals were starting to fill up with cases in the cities. Out here in the rural areas there were no cases yet.

Like other strains of the virus we have seen in the past, said the announcer, it appears that some people can carry the illness without showing symptoms. Others are highly susceptible.

Someone groaned. "Not another virus," she said.

Over the last few decades there had been numerous pandemics associated with a particularly nasty mutating virus.

"We should have a meeting," said another. "Come up with a community plan."

"Calm down everyone," said Basquiat. "We'll get through this."

The lengthening shadows of fall finally began to creep into warm evenings. Lyra was anxious thinking about Inas, who would be needing help bringing in the harvest. The news about the virus—Rosie Sickness, people were calling it, because it turned your face red—got worse. The mounting death count meant that the regime's downplay of the virus was wearing thin. Lyra started to worry about Papa Gilles, and Sayre, and Inas, and everyone else back in Dummer. Her family members were the kind of people who would listen to the regime's broadcast. The oligarchs didn't want to pay for healthcare.

Although they tried to reduce contact with potentially sick outsiders, one day someone at the Androscoggin Free Zone started coughing. Then suddenly a lot of people were coughing. Only a couple of them got the red face. One person sweated and screamed all night, suffering from frightful hallucinations.

"Hard times in the Kingdom of Coos," said Basquiat.

Even Basquiat was sick, spending a whole week in his bed.

Everyone in the free zone recovered eventually, but they were left weak, as though the Rosie had sucked the life out of them, but not all the way. The man who painfully hallucinated had a look of permanent haunting.

After he recovered, Basquiat was worried about Inas. He found Lyra.

"I'm going to visit Auntie Inas. I think it's about time you got back to your folks right? Won't they be worried about you?"

"No," lied Lyra. "But I am worried about Inas too. She has no one to take in the harvest."

"What do you say we head out there in a few days?"

"Okay."

Lyra knew this day would come, but still it came as a surprise. She missed her family, even though she had her issues with them. She didn't think she could just live in Dummer forever, but she did want to see them. She knew she would miss Glinda most of all. Sure, she could come and visit, or even come live here one day, but Lyra had been taught by life so far that when something good happens to you, enjoy it as much in the moment as you can, because that one moment will never happen again. She couldn't bring herself to quite say goodbye, but she cuddled into Glinda's bed with her the night before she left. In the morning she slipped away quietly before Glinda woke up, and left her fringe jacket folded beside the bed as a gift.

Sikivu decided to come along with Lyra and Basquiat.

"Dummer is boring," said Lyra, but secretly she was glad Sikivu was coming. She was interesting and when she spoke Lyra learned things.

"What is mundane to you is fascinating to me," said the filmmaker. "So I'm looking forward to it."

Lyra pulled her bicycle out of hiding and they were off.

"Why did you call it the Androscoggin Free Zone?" Lyra called out to Basquiat as she zoomed by on her bicycle, Starlight running around her in circles.

"Androscoggin is the name of the river close by. The strip mall is part of Milan Town, which got a lot of tourist visitors because it was on the Appalachian Trail, but when the train stopped running gas car was the only way to get in. The place is just about a ghost town these days."

"Inspiring," said Lyra with a deadpan expression. Sikivu laughed. Lyra noticed that the camera was probably rolling, tucked nonchalantly under her arm.

As they journeyed Lyra noticed that the leaves were shifting from rich green to yellow in some places. Fall was coming.

From the distance Lyra could see a massive pile of twisted junk by the roadside.

"We're getting close," she said.

They turned off the main road into Dummer Mobile Home Park and went around to visit Inas first.

"You go on ahead," said Lyra. "I'll be right there."

Lyra had to stash her bike. She detoured to her usual spot. There was a thicket of bushes beside a pile of junk. She slid the bike inside and covered it with a tattered old piece of black vapour-guard, making sure none of it was visible to passers-by. Then she made her way to Inas'.

When she arrived, Bas was talking to her through the door. She was quarantining. She had not been sick but the sickness ripped through the area and a lot of people were still suffering.

Lyra slid up close to the window and peered inside. Inas cackled at her.

"Fancy seeing you!"

"I'm sorry I was gone so long Inas," said Lyra. She hated uncomfortable conversations but she really felt bad about not helping with the gardens.

"No matter. I'm glad to see you."

"This is Sikivu," said Bas, introducing the filmmaker. "She's been staying at the Free Zone and she wanted to come along."

"You took my little friend and now you've brought me a woman to meet," said Inas, winking at Lyra.

Lyra turned to see Sikivu and Bas both laugh a little and avoid each others' gaze and she noticed something she never had before; there was some kind of secret between them.

"Well, ah, sorry, Auntie…" began Bas awkwardly.

"All right, all right… go fetch me some leeks. They're way off in that wet bed and I've missed them in my soup." She turned to Lyra. "Show them where that is, will you?”

Lyra nodded and darted off to the shed to get the tools. She grabbed the wheelbarrow. “We’ll need this,” she said to the others.

When they got to Inas’ far patches, Lyra saw that they were not in great shape. Weeds were growing high and choking out the carrots. The dill grew high and strong though. Lyra set to work on her hands and knees plucking weeds. She noticed that there was a large hole in the fence and rabbits had gotten in.

“Fix up that hole,” she said quietly. Basquiat set to work. Sikivu didn’t know what was a weed and didn’t want to get her hands dirty, so she filmed closeups of their hands as they worked.
The hours passed quickly. Lyra always felt like time spent in the garden was the best feeling, second only to painting. The weed pile was high. Finally she stood back to survey what they had done. It looked much better than before.

“I’ll have to come back to this tomorrow,” said Lyra. “There’s more to do. But this looks pretty good.”

They filled the wheelbarrow with leeks and other fresh treats and went back to Inas’ house.

They washed the vegetables with the hand pump in the yard and then left them there for Inas to gather later.

“I love you Auntie,” said Bas. “We’re going to head back home okay? I wish we could stay for soup.”

“Love you too,” said Inas. She was sad they couldn’t stay either. They blew kisses through the door and then Bas and Sikivu took their leave.

“Bring her back when the sickness is over,” called Inas as they left. Sikivu smiled and waved goodbye.

“And I’ll see you tomorrow,” said Inas to Lyra.

“See you tomorrow,” said Lyra, gathering up a few vegetables for dinner.

She headed into Dummer.

CHAPTER 7: Lyra

Lyra walked into Dummer Mobile Home Park to find a strange energy pervading the air. Everyone was locked up inside. She made her way to the trailer where she had spent most of her life. She opened the door.

"Come on Starlight," she called, but the dog would not go inside.

Lyra found Papa Gilles lying on the front bed slack-jawed and sweating in grimy sheets. The place stank of illness. She made her way to the back compartment, where Sayre was also pale and clammy in bed with the curtains drawn.

"I'm home," she whispered. She didn't want to disturb their rest but she also suddenly desperately wanted a hug. She felt emotion prick the corners of her eyes. She shook herself out of it and went back outside.

Lyra set to work getting the cooking fire going. She would make them something to eat, at least. Part of her felt like they would be angry about her long absence. She set little potatoes to boil, and she would add onions and leeks after. She wondered if there were eggs. She went quietly into the trailer and checked the food stores. There was not a scrap to be found.

Thank goodness they had the smoked fish, thought Lyra. She felt a pang of guilt for being away so long.

"Lyra?" said Sayre weakly from the back room.

"Yes, mama."

Lyra appeared in the doorway. Sayre sat up weakly in bed.

"I knew you'd come back. I was worried sick. Come here."

Lyra went in for a hug. She felt the hard roundness of Sayre's belly. She was pregnant.

Sayre coughed. It was an awful sound. Her cheeks were fiery red.

"You got the Rosie mama," said Lyra.

"Yes, you shouldn't be in here…" she trailed off and let herself fall back into the pillow.

"Well it's too late for that now. I'm making dinner for us." Lyra turned to leave, and Sayre let out a pitiful sound.

"Please, don't leave…"

"I'll be back. You need something to eat."

"I'm so hungry…" said Sayre as Lyra left the trailer.

Dinner was almost cooked. As Lyra stirred the pan, she felt a prickle up her spine. She looked around out of the corners of her eyes and noticed people watching her through their dark windows.

They're probably hungry too, she thought.

"Starlight," she called softly. The dog padded over from under the trailer and sat beside her. Lyra scratched her head.

This isn't like the Androscoggin Free Zone, she thought. Everyone there had taken care of each other in sickness.

She took the pan into the trailer and fixed up two plates.

"Mama, dinner's ready," she said softly into Sayre's

bedroom.

Lyra walked over to Papa Gilles. He looked so vulnerable lying there sleeping.

He looks old, she thought.

She stroked his shoulder gently.

"Papa," she whispered. "Dinner's ready."

He didn't move. She shook him a little. He needed sleep but he needed to eat too.

He groaned a little in his sleep. Lyra shook him a little harder.

"Papa, food…."

He breathed hard and then coughed himself awake.

"Lyra?" he said, squinting at her.

"Yes Papa Gilles. Come to the table."

She helped him sit up. His greasy hair stood right up on his head.

"Come," she said, guiding him over and sitting him down at a plate. "Eat."

Sayre came and sat across from him.

"What about you Lyra?" she said.

"Don't worry about me, I had a big breakfast." It was true. She had a full egg and toast breakfast this morning before they left.

I guess I'm back to one meal a day, she thought.

"I'm sorry there's no food," said Sayre weakly.

"Damn hooligans been raiding trailers while sick people are sleeping," coughed Papa Gilles. He was starting to wake up but he looked pale as a ghost.

"I wish Brandon was here," said Sayre.

"Would he really be any help right now?" said Lyra coldly.

Sayre looked at her with tired eyes.

"I know you and your brother don't get along right now… that's just because you're kids. One day you'll appreciate one another. And one day he'll be brave and strong, and he'll protect us… you'll appreciate him then."

Lyra remembered her last interaction with her brother and shuddered at the thought of Brandon strong.

Sayre and Papa Gilles ate up their entire plates and went back to bed.

The next day Lyra made Papa Gilles move to the back compartment with Sayre.

"I'm cleaning your sheets," she said. "It stinks in here."

He didn't argue, or even grumble. Lyra knew he must really be sick.

She stripped the bed and realized that Gilles must have pissed himself in there too. She carried everything to the pump and did her best to soak and squeeze the sweat out of it as best she could. It was not as good as Sayre would do it, but it would have to do for now.

She laid the bedclothes out in the sun outside the trailer. A cool breeze whipped around the campground. Lyra looked at the trees in the distance. There were now oranges amid the yellows and greens. Lyra realized that there was a lot to do to prepare for winter.

In the afternoon she trudged over to Inas' and worked in the garden until her fingers were sore. It was hard work but it felt good to be helping. After seeing Sayre and Papa Gilles, she was glad that Inas was isolating. She didn't even knock on the door.

Her stomach was soon grumbling with hunger. She realized that she had gotten used to eating two meals a day instead of one. She used to be able to get by on so little. She plucked a handful of the abundant tomatoes and a cucumber. She wondered if the corn was about ready to take in and prepare for winter. She sniffed the air. No frosts yet.

Lyra harvested a whole wheelbarrow of crops. She parked it beside the house for Inas to take in and prepare. Lyra was sad that she wouldn't get to stand beside Inas in the kitchen cutting and spicing the pickles, or making chutneys for the winter. She wondered how long the Rosie would last. She soaked herself with the hand pump, letting all the dirt wash away.

When she got back to the trailer, the sheets looked about dry in the afternoon sun. She went inside and rooted around for something dry to wear. All her old clothes looked too small.

"You've grown," said Sayre quietly. She was awake, wrapped in a blanket and smoking.

"Should you really be doing that?" asked Lyra.

Sayre just laughed, and it turned into a nasty cough. Then she got up and pulled out an old sweater of hers.

"Try this on," she said.

Lyra pulled off her wet shirt and put on the sweater. It fit.

"You're adult sized," said Sayre with surprise. "My little girl runs off and this woman comes back to me. What have you been up to?"

"I met some nice people. Some bad ones too, I guess," said Lyra, thinking on it, "but I had Starlight so it was okay."

"Well I'm glad to hear that," said Sayre.

After a long pause, Lyra spoke.

"What do you think I should do with my life?" she asked.

Sayre looked at her with non-comprehension.

"You're doing it, sweetie."

Most people are born into a world of the expectations of others. Lyra was not, and that had its difficulties too.

Sayre and Lyra made the front bed.

"Thank you," said Sayre. "I would have cleaned them, but…"

"Don't worry mum. It's okay."

Sayre helped Lyra strip the rest of the beds. They opened every window and aired the sickness out of the trailer. Papa Gilles got up and fussed around a bit. His energy was low, but he looked better than he had on Lyra's return. He and Sayre both sat wrapped in blankets at the table while Lyra brought them fresh vegetables. They ate them without complaint, even though Papa Gilles preferred to eat everything cooked.

"The living plant has good nutrients," said Lyra. "It'll help you get better." Glinda had told her that. She was something called a 'raw vegan.'

"You sound like a merde granola," said Gilles, but he ate his veggies.

Lyra found out that Mustang Dougie had died of the Rosie. So had some others. His trailer had been torn apart by scavengers. Papa Gilles had helped to bury his body before he himself got sick.

Lyra helped Inas get the rest of the crops in. There were long days in the field and Lyra's hands developed calluses from the rake and shovel. A few good frost days came and went, and the trees declined in fireworks of red and gold. Piles of leaves blanketed the ground beneath baring trees and the smell of death saturated the air like a heavy perfume. Winter was coming.

Far away in the Capitol, the President had declared himself Supreme Leader of the Republic. This was the second time in the country's history. This Supreme Leader was much the same as his uncle who first claimed the title, the tyrant who served for four terms because he refused to leave. That had scared enough people to vote Democrat, and in the interim there had been a Democratic government, but they were not brave and did not make any systemic changes necessary to safeguard the people's government against oligarchs, and build a future for the nation's people, so the first Supreme Leader's nephew was now the new Supreme Leader. It was a parody of the last days of Ancient Rome, to anyone who even knew what that meant anymore.

The United States political system in general pit two groups against one another, creating a small civil war every election. Socialism in much of the rest of the world gradually created a middle class, multiple political parties and normalized coalition governments, collaborative discourse, and fostered stability. Stability itself was antithetical to the boom and bust of the modern capitalist system. Countries working on building stable social

frameworks and local economies principled by equity
were moving into a new global paradigm, while some
gripped by oil and corporate interests were being sucked
dry and left behind. Partisan movements blossomed
into multiple factions that created diverse new political
parties, both of the Leftish and Rightish orientations, all
over the world. America though was stuck stagnating in
a two-party system. What was considered right-wing in
Canada, for example, would be far left in USA, because
multiple parties allowed for more fulsome debate and
representation. The two party system worked like this:
so-called Democrats were ruled by a wealthy corporate-
backed elite who never really wanted to change the status
quo, and the People's Left had no leverage in a two-party
system. The ruling circle of the Democrats was not
made of working class people. Only occasionally would
measures get pushed through to support the working
class. The so-called Republican party was a pulpit for
demagogues, who would get elected when the peasants
were fed up with bad government bread crumbs. The
two-party system meant disappointing, inadequate,
moderately corrupt Democratic government terms,
interspersed with periods of utter chaos and extreme
corruption by increasingly unhinged Republican regimes.

Here in Dummer Mobile Home Park, this or that
Supreme Leader felt the same as a Democratic leader. In
fact, Supreme Leaders were more entertaining, especially
during a crisis like Rosie Sickness, when even the so-
called Democrats would not be providing public care
anyway.

The Mormon Proctors declared themselves supreme
leaders in their own right, resurrecting their old vestigial
Territory of Deseret boundaries to claim sovereignty.
They had an arrangement with the Care Pastors to
provide medical care in their State that was so powerful it
created a Great Schism in the Care Movement and a new
Care Seminary was established in Deseret.

One township over from Androscoggin Free Zone,

in Oxford County, a syndicate of wealthy landowners had declared themselves Lords and established an autonomous state called Gilead. The upper circle of leaders, key members of the Fraternity, lived lavish lifestyles and inflicted Draconian measures of control over the populace, and women in particular.

On the other hand, the Free Zone movement flourished, with hundreds of communities taking off.

The Act of the Union to create United States pulled apart at the seams the way it was knitted together, with a mosaic of micro-utopias and micro-dystopias.

A second wave of the Rosie struck Dummer Mobile Home Park. After the first wave did so much damage, word went around that they would strive for quarantine. People constructed face masks out of old rags to reduce the spread of contagion when outside their homes. People avoided direct physical contact with one another. Now that many had recovered, proper services were held for the dead. The Park came together for a community meeting and developed a sanitation policy. There were people who just continued living as usual, maskless, without regard for reducing the spread, and those people were shunned into compliance. The Park became a community. Lyra spoke up at the meetings and offered her experience in Androscoggin Free Zone to show that there were better ways. She was surprised to find that after the death of the loud and self-serving Mustang Dougie, there were other quieter people in the community with good ideas who actually made decent leaders.

Then winter came.

One cold day followed another and the next morning they woke up to a fine layer of snow coating the tops of trailers and the dirt roads between them. The snow melted by the afternoon but in the evening fat flakes began to fall and they filled the air all night. In the morning the snow was deep enough to step on without the mud soaking through.

Lyra felt trapped inside the small trailer this winter

for the first time ever. She imagined what winter was like in the cabin where Papa Gilles grew up, or the Androscoggin Free Zone. She tried to imagine winter in Goreham City but she couldn't.

Despite their precautions and care, many people got sick again. The community was strained—at night Lyra could hear the sounds of domestic violence from the trailer beside theirs. Sometimes it got so bad it scared her, but what could anyone do? There was no women's shelter and no one wanted the extra mouths to feed of the young children living there. Lyra slipped them a jar of Inas' chutney. She imagined that hunger was a factor in the strain.

One particularly dark and cold day, Brandon appeared at the trailer. He had shot up past six feet tall and there was a large healing gash on his forehead that made him look older.

"Grease Lightnin!" shouted Lyra as the dog ran up the road behind him. Starlight shot out from under the trailer and the dogs greeted one another with kisses and head bumps. Grease Lightnin was huge.

"Monster, come here!" yelled Brandon, who had renamed him Monster. The dog ignored him.

"Brandon!" Sayre came out of the house wrapped in a blanket and threw her arms around him. She pulled his head down and kissed his cheeks.

"Look at you, all grown up," she said.

"Okay, Sayre, relax," he said.

"Sayre? Baby what's wrong?" she cried.

"Mum," he said quietly, "everything's fine."

"The Dummer Boyz run you off?" said Lyra.

Brandon sneered at her.

"Don't call me Sayre, Brandon."

She pulled him into the house.

"Gilles! Look who's back!"

Papa Gilles grunted a hello.

It suddenly felt very tight in the trailer with Brandon and Lyra so big. They weren't little kids running around anymore. Brandon's legs would probably hang off the end of his fold-up bed now.

"You stickin around?" asked Gilles.

"Gilles!" scolded Sayre. "Of course he is!" She clutched Brandon's arm as though he were going to leave any second.

"Look at him, he's a man now, he can do what he wants," said Gilles.

Lyra rolled her eyes.

"Things are going to be so great now that you're back," said Sayre.

"Sure mum," he said. He sat down on his bed, the couch area of the trailer. Lyra stared at him with her piercing eyes.

He looks haunted, she thought.

"What happened to your forehead?" she asked quietly.

"Shh, Lyra leave him alone," said Sayre. She would rather not know.

"Life on the road," said Brandon with a shrug.

"Would you like something to eat?" said Sayre, not that there was much to eat. There were fresh eggs from Inas' chickens at least.

"Sure," he said.

She set to work getting the pan ready.

The eggs that were to last a few days were quickly gone.

"We're celebrating," said Sayre. "I'll get us more food, don't worry."

The day was over early. The nights were long and cold. Winter's peak was still coming.

"Here sweetie, you can have my bed tonight," said Sayre. "I'll sleep here." She sat down beside him on his little couch bed.

"Thanks," he said, getting up and going into the back of the trailer.

Sayre stretched out on the little couch and wrapped her blanket tighter around her, stretching it over her pregnant belly. It was going to be a cold night.

That night Lyra was quite warm sleeping beside Papa Gilles. He was like a big furnace, and this part of the trailer was insulated. She was restless though and kept waking up all night. She felt out of place here, like she was always tagging along or fighting for a little corner of her own. There wasn't even a bed for her here. She loved but also resented her family.

Even Brandon had no place to grow here and had to join the stupid Dummer Boyz to get out, she thought. Even though they had their differences, she was sad to see his face cut up like that and she hoped whatever happened wasn't too awful.

She wondered how Glinda was doing at Androscoggin Free Zone. She thought back on summer and wished she was spending her day painting at one of those big trestle tables. Even there she did not totally fit in. She thought about visiting one of the big cities to see what it was like.

Starlight wouldn't like it there, she thought.

She wondered what Joan Whiteduck was doing right now. She imagined that whatever it was, it must be glorious.

Maybe she has a cool activist headquarters where she lives with all her cool activist friends, thought Lyra. She remembered how confident Joan was walking up onto the stage in the town square of Randolph. She made a note to charge her phone so she could look up where Joan lived. She hadn't been online since she was back in Dummer. She wanted to check in on Basquiat and the Free Zone too.

The next day there was a massive storm. Snow piled up past the bottom of the trailer door. The sun came out for a short time and children built forts out of snow.

"Are you going to play with them honey?" asked Sayre.

Lyra looked at her with her big guarded eyes, hiding her thoughts.

Maybe I will, she thought. *Maybe I'll build a house of out snow...* She had seen in a book that Inuit people built houses out of snow. She would be scared to fall asleep in there in case she was buried alive, or accidentally froze to death. There was a science to it, she was sure, but she didn't have the teachings.

Another storm wave hit that lasted for days. They were trapped indoors with just each others' company. Brandon and Lyra started sniping at each other and it was almost unbearable. Cruel words were exchanged. Lyra thought more seriously about her snow house, and the sting of resentment for her family grew more acute.

"There's no food," yelled Brandon one sharply cold afternoon.

"I haven't had a chance to get out," said Sayre. She was still not completely recovered from her battle with the Rosie. She needed a few good weeks of sunshine to warm her bones.

"You could get off your ass and help out, calisse," growled Papa Gilles. They were all getting on each others' nerves.

Sayre left the trailer for a few days. When she came back, she had a sack of split peas, a bag of powdered milk, and a few packs of cigarettes. Brandon swiped a pack.

"Hey!" said Sayre. "You're too young for those."

He laughed and lit one up.

"I said no!" she shouted.

He ignored her completely.

"Don't smoke in here," said Lyra, disgusted.

Brandon just blew clouds in her direction.

Sayre made a huge pot of split pea soup that lasted for days. They still had salt from Papa Gilles' trade at the General Store in Randolph. Gilles was feeling better now and both he and Sayre were out a lot, making things work for the family.

Soon enough Sayre was coughing again. The sound started deep in her chest like a rattle and then rumbled out so hard it burst blood vessels in her cheeks, turning them bright red.

"Stay in bed mother," said Lyra. "It'll only get worse. We'll manage."

Lyra confined her to the back compartment of the trailer. The last thing they wanted was to get Papa Gilles sick too.

The Rosie spread like wildfire through the camp again. The sounds of sickness could be heard day and night. Lyra could hardly sleep because the neighbours were worse than ever. At least twice a week there was an eruption of violence. The howls of suffering rose and fell like a chorus of coyotes, the mother a keen painful cry and the children the yips and refrain amidst the whistle and susurration of winter winds in the night.

Papa Gilles spent more of his nights out drinking hooch at the Pickled Peach than in the trailer. His hair was thinning and his skin turned sallow. His eyes looked dull from the booze that never quite had a chance to leave his system. It was his coping mechanism.

One day, Brandon disappeared, and Monster with him. They simply left.

Lyra decided to go to the Pickled Peach with Papa Gilles to charge her phone. She hated it there because the old men were disgusting, and even moreso now that she was older, but she wanted to see what was happening in the world. She frowned and slipped Papa Gilles' special bone-handled knife into her bag just case. She went inside and sat on the floor in the corner, willing herself not to be noticed by the old grimy charging plug.

"Ehhh, girly," said Old Jean.

Lyra frowned and looked at him.

"You look like you're growing up fine…" he leaned closer, almost falling over. "When are you gunna start paying for that like your mother does?"

She scowled at him and willed herself to blend into

the wall. She wished she could make herself invisible. The knife she knew was in her bag gave her comfort.

"Ta guelle!" said Papa Gilles sharply. He didn't hear what was said but he could tell it wasn't good. 'Ta guelle' was something French you say to a dog to make it stop barking. Old Jean grinned at her and dissolved into drunken laughter. Then he went back to his bottle.

Lyra learned from the news that this was one of the coldest winters in the remembered history of the region. People were freezing to death in their homes in many of the small communities where the trees had been stripped long ago and they were without reliable heat. Lyra knew that even in Dummer some of the trailers weren't insulated. A couple hours south, the Goreham Hospital was letting people camp out. They got flooded with the Rosie, and some people never left. There was a little tent city outside and doctors inside were converting rooms into temporary housing. Even some people who weren't sick were making a pilgrimage to the hospital to shelter from the winter cold. Joan Whiteduck was travelling by dogsled on a tour of affected communities in her traditional territory. She donned a bodysuit soaked in blood and made snow angels to discordant live music in protest. It was all filmed by drone and broadcast around the world.

Lyra unplugged and turned off her phone. When she came back to reality, she remembered that she was sitting on the floor of a broken down trailer bar getting catcalled by dirty old men. She shivered. There was a draft creeping into her bones. It was time to go home. She looked at Papa Gilles. He was so stone drunk he didn't even seem to recognize her. She stood up and brushed herself off. She steeled herself against the cold and charged out the door of the trailer into the night.

The air was perfectly clear and deadly cold. Lyra looked up at the cloud of white her breath made in a swirl around her head. She clutched her faded jacket tighter around her and held her breath. The Milky Way was a crust of glittering contrast against the deep dark. Someone in Dummer told her once that the sky was a big blanket full of pinpricks and there was an alien up there called the Almighty who was shining a light behind it and that's what stars were. Lyra knew that wasn't true but she could imagine it tonight.

When she got back to the trailer she pulled on her warm fleece pants and cozy socks and wrapped herself up as tight as she could and went to sleep.

CHAPTER 8: Lyra and Sayre

Lyra woke up suddenly to the sound of screams. She was warm; strangely warm. She blinked hard and looked around groggily. She didn't feel like she had slept long but it was oddly bright outside. Sayre stumbled out of the back of the trailer, pulling on her boots.

"Fire!" The word came out in a strangled cry.

Lyra sat up straight, suddenly awake. She pulled on her coat and grabbed her satchel.

"Come on!" screamed Sayre. The air felt hot and Lyra could smell smoke and burning plastic. She shook her head awake and plunged her feet into her boots.

Sayre was shaking Papa Gilles. He was passed out hard on the bed snoring with his mouth wide open. He didn't move an inch.

Lyra joined her, pulling his arms and legs with all her might, but he was a heavy man, and when he drank like this nothing could wake him.

The trailer door burst open and a neighbour's face popped inside.

"Get out of here! Fire!"

Sayre and Lyra were both screaming now, their voices joining the chorus of suffering all around them.

"Go!" screamed Sayre at Lyra. "Go!"

"I'm not leaving you!" said Lyra.

"Help!" screamed Sayre. "Go get help!"

Lyra went outside and stumbled around the snow. It was a frenzy of chaos outside. The flames danced high, blinding her momentarily. The whole park was on fire. All the little houses and sheds crowded together were crashing and melting before her eyes.

"Help!" she screamed. "Help!"

No one heard her. Everyone was entrenched in their own struggle to survive the inferno.

Lyra went back inside.

"There's no one," she screamed.

Sayre started coughing. The smoke was thick and acrid now. Lyra's eyes stung so bad she could barely see. The curtains were on fire now.

Sayre fell to her knees, struggling to breathe. Papa Gilles was out cold.

Lyra tried one more time to rouse him, shaking him as hard as she could. She slapped his face and screamed in his ear. Finally she grabbed Sayre's arm and dragged her out.

"I love you Papa," she shouted behind her through ragged breaths, tears rolling down her face. There was a crash inside. The trailer was collapsing.

Sayre and Lyra stumbled down the road and out of the park, joining the other survivors on the outskirts of town, watching their lives burn away.

The fire started easily enough—someone very cold constructed a woodstove in their trailer out of scrap metal and fell asleep. It could have happened to anyone. The whole park was a ramshackle tinderbox of questionable building standards.

Three people died in the fire, including Papa Gilles, and many more had burn injuries. Half the trailer park

burned to the ground. It looked an awful carnage, until
the first snow mercifully veiled the burned wreckage
in white. Some folks were able to bunk into surviving
trailers, but there was not enough room for everyone.

"I know a place I can go," said Sayre. "But I don't
know if it's safe for you…"

"I can go to Inas'," said Lyra. "But what about you?
How can it be safe for you if it isn't safe for me?"

Sayre was silent. She looked Lyra up and down.
The quiet little girl was gone and a young lady stood
before her, a thirteen-year-old whose womanly figure was
beginning to emerge in hints of hips and breasts and fuller
lips.

"It's a client," she said, finally. "I don't want that
for you." She reached out and touched Lyra's soft cheek.
"Please tell Inas I'm grateful."

Lyra held her mother tight.

"Be careful," she said, as though she were the mother
and Sayre were the daughter.

Lyra trudged through the snow to Inas' house with
Starlight alongside her. She saw the scars on Starlight's
face and shoulders and remembered the burn marks when
they first met.

"You've been through this before," said Lyra.

Starlight shot off across the snow. A few minutes
later she came trotting back with a white rabbit in her
jowls.

"You're a survivor," said Lyra. She wiped tears
from her eyes. She didn't know why she was crying,
even though she had plenty of reasons. She just felt
overwhelmed by emotion. "Thank you for being my
friend," she said, scratching the dog affectionately behind
the ears. Starlight tossed the little rabbit corpse in the air
and snapped it nearly in two with one big chomp of her
grisly jowls.

As they got closer to Inas' house, Lyra heard a
strange man's voice. She frowned and crouched into a

fight-or-flight stance. The muscles on Starlight's neck popped out and her head ducked low. They prowled closer. Lyra heard the smash of glass, and a wail in Inas' voice.

"Get away!" said Inas.

"Go get him!" cried Lyra, pointing to the man breaking into Inas' door. Starlight shot forward, her shoulders rippling with muscle. She let out a fearsome series of rumbling barks. The man turned just in time for Lyra to see that it was her neighbour. His family's trailer had burned to the ground just like hers. Starlight took him down in seconds, her sheer weight pinning him and her massive jaws ripping out his throat before another word could be said. His blood sprayed a river of crimson into the snow. Inas was crying inside.

"I'm sorry," cried Lyra, not sure who she was talking to. "I'm sorry… I'm sorry…"

"Come inside, come on, come inside," said Inas, pulling her in and closing the door behind her.

"I'm sorry Inas," said Lyra, tears running streaks down her dirty face.

"Nevermind child. nevermind…" said Inas, bringing her a damp towel.

Lyra held the towel over her face for a moment, catching her breath. Then she wiped away the soot and grime. Inas brought over a bowl of soup. She made up a bowl for Starlight too.

"Here you go beastie," she said, leaving the bowl outside the door, trying to avoid looking at the lifeless body in the snow.
A cold wind blew in through the broken window in the door.

"Let me fix that," said Lyra.

Inas stuffed the hole with a tablecloth. It didn't stop the draft completely but it helped a lot.

"Let's worry about that later," said the old woman. "For now, eat your soup."

Lyra didn't argue. She spooned the vegetables into

her mouth and then drained the broth. Inas hummed along with the old hand-crank radio.

"Now then," said Inas. "Let's get that man out of here."

Lyra nodded.

"We gotta get him into the wheelbarrow. Then you can take him to the woods somewhere."

"Won't someone see him?" asked Lyra.

"It's been a cold winter," said Inas. "The animals will find him first."

Lyra shivered at the thought of his corpse being picked away by ravens and wolverines. Inas was right. There were creatures that would welcome the meat on his bones.

They bundled up warm and went out into the snow. The sun was setting.

The man was heavy but between them they were able to get him into the wheelbarrow. He was already cold to the touch, his life warmth drained away like the blood from his throat.

"It'll be hard going my girlie, but you can do it."

Inas went back inside. Lyra gripped the handles of the wheelbarrow and pushed with all her might. It wasn't that bad close to the house where the snow had been stomped down, but out further it was almost impossible. Lyra didn't know how she would be able to get him into the woods. She took him as far as she could muster, dug a little trench in the snow with her mittened hands, and dumped him into it. She kicked snow back over him, attempting to cover him as best she could. It was not nearly as far away as she wanted to take him, but it was all she could do.

"Rest in peace." She didn't know what else to say.

By the time Lyra pushed the wheelbarrow back into Inas' shed it was pitch black outside. Lyra went inside the house and stomped the snow from her feet. Inas had made her up a little resting place on the floor by the woodstove. Inas herself slept on a cot in the kitchen where the winds whistling through the drafty old house were not as cold.

Lyra stayed with Inas for the next few days. She told her everything that had happened. She told her about Papa Gilles, the fire, Sayre, and the neighbour man's wife and children crying all night. Now he would never come home. Inas ladled them more soup. Starlight even came inside the house and slept curled up with Lyra on the floor.

Inas got out the tools and Lyra boarded up the broken door.

"I'm worried about my mother," said Lyra.

"Sounds like it," said Inas. She would not tell Lyra what to do.

Finally Lyra decided that she had to see Sayre. She would keep her distance, just to avoid the Rosie, but she wanted to make sure her mother was okay.

Lyra walked back into Dummer Mobile Home Park. She felt a pang in her heart at the sight of the empty space where their trailer had been. The Pickled Peach was stained black with smoke, but it had survived the fire. She went inside.

"Does anyone know where Sayre is?" she asked, staying a few metres away from the men sitting at the crudely built bar.

"She was at Francis' place, but then she got sick and he gave her the boot. Try Dirt Row."

Lyra left and walked down to the other side of the trailer park where a series of sheds and shacks in various states of deterioration were cobbled together. Lyra could hear the soft rise and fall of many voices, and coughing. She held her breath and peered inside. She squinted as her eyes adjusted to the dimly lit interior.

"Excuse me," she said, as someone sleeping in a pile of blankets by the door scowled at the bright light shining on her face.

"Close the door!"

Lyra nipped in and shut the door. The place was full.

Every corner was occupied. Old clothes and blankets lay on the pallets lining the dirt floor. There were makeshift clotheslines and privacy curtains strung across the room. Lyra could smell the reek of sickness.

"Sayre!" she called somewhat softly. Then louder: "Sayre!"

She realized that if she wanted to find Sayre then she would have to go inside, and she would not be able to go back to Inas' house and risk transmitting the Rosie. She sighed and stepped forward. She had a bad feeling that she could not ignore.

Lyra Muse walked from room to room on the labyrinthine path through the shacks, winding her way around her displaced community crammed in with the kind folks of Dirt Row who took them in.

Suddenly she saw the familiar face of her mother. Sayre was lying on the floor in the same clothes Lyra had seen her in last. Her pregnant belly was big enough now that she lay on her side, one hand holding her stomach.

"Mumma?" said Lyra, running over to her.

Sayre looked up, and when she saw Lyra she got to her feet.

"Lyra!" she said. Then she pushed her away. "I'm sick. You'll have to stay away from me," she said.

Lyra looked her mother up and down. Despite her round belly, she was thinner than Lyra had ever seen her in the shoulders and face. Her hair was greasy and her clothes were still blotted with soot from the fire.

"You're not okay mum," said Lyra quietly. "When was the last time you ate?"

"I ate yesterday," said Sayre without conviction.

"They're taking people in, down at Goreham Hospital. Let's go. They can get you treatment for the Rosie, food, a warm place to stay for the winter…"

"Leave Dummer?" Sayre looked filled with doubt.

"There's nothing left!" said Lyra, looking around. She raised her voice. "We are going up to Goreham Hospital. They have rooms there for people to spend this bad winter, and medicine. Anyone who wants to come, we're leaving this afternoon. It's a long walk, you'll need boots."

A few people looked up. There were whispers between people.

"You can come back and help rebuild in the spring if you want," said Lyra gently to her mother. "But we need to go now while you still have the strength to get there."

Sayre started coughing. It was the rattle deep in her chest. Her cheeks fired red.

Up against a nearby wall sat the woman who lived in the trailer next door, surrounded by four children. It was the family of the man who had broken into Inas' house, the man whose body Lyra had dumped by the roadside. She looked like she wanted to say something.

"Come with us," said Lyra to her. "Please."

The woman looked like she had been crying. The children were hungry, as usual.

"We lost Gus in the fire," said the woman, Claudette. "I don't know what to do."

"Come with us," said Lyra gently. "There is a better life for us than this. Come."

The woman nodded.

"Gather your things, get as many warm clothes on as you can. I'll be back soon and we'll leave this afternoon."

Lyra hurried back to Inas' house. She knocked on the door.

"Don't come out Inas," she called. "My mother's got the Rosie again."

"Lyra. What are you going to do?"

"Just hand me my things please… I'm taking her to Goreham Hospital. They got warm beds and food up there."

"I know," said Inas. "I heard it on the radio." Inas went inside and gathered up Lyra's satchel and prepared a packet of preserves.

"Be careful," she said, leaving it on the step for Lyra

to take with her.

"Thank you Inas."

Lyra decided to leave her bicycle in hiding and Starlight with Inas. She didn't want to travel without Starlight by her side, but she didn't know if town would be safe for the dog.

I doubt they would let her into the hospital, thought Lyra. *And it will be safer for Inas with Starlight here.*

She walked down the road back to Dirt Row to get her mother and the others.

The rag-taggle bunch walked along the snowy road out of Dummer. It was hard going until they got onto the highway, which was more or less walkable from the big trucks and the wind blowing away the snow.

"How far is it?" asked Sayre, looking at the little ones already slowing down.

"Two hours."

It took over three hours to reach the snow-covered town. Lyra had passed by this way to get to Androscoggin Free Zone, but the others had never left Dummer and they were awestruck.

As they approached the hospital, they could see that a huge shacktown had been constructed here too. There were barrel fires interspersed amongst what looked like dozens, or even a hundred tents. Police officers guarded the hospital entrance.

The Dummer pilgrims walked up to the large doors.

"We're sick," said Lyra. "We need to get into the hospital, please." She was fairly certain that telling the officers they planned to stay here and never leave was not the right approach, considering the large crowd camped out here.

The officers eyed the group of women and children. A baby unlatched from Claudette's breast and started to cry. As if on cue, Sayre let out an eruption of coughing.

"Please sir, we need help," whispered Claudette. The children shivered.

"Go on in," said one of the officers. The other one rolled his eyes but stepped aside. The automatic doors swooshed open and the children gasped with surprise. They went inside.

It was just a dingy small town hospital, but to the Dummer folks it looked like a fancy hotel. There were matching chairs all in a row, posters on the clean gray walls, and hospital staff bustling around in uniforms. Multiple screens showed the news, television interviews, and even a Christmas special.

"I'm glad we came," said Alexandra, Claudette's eldest daughter. The children gravitated over to the screens.

An employee came over to them dressed in protective equipment, including a mask and face shield.

"Which one of you is the patient today?" she said politely, looking over the group. Several children had runny noses. Her eyes landed on Sayre, whose cheeks were bright red.

"All of us, I think," said Claudette softly.

"What happened to you?"

Claudette laughed. It was a strange and painful sound.

"What happened to us?" she repeated, her eyes faraway.

"Our home burned down," said Lyra quickly, stepping forward. "And some of us may have the Rosie."

"Your house burned down? When did that occur?" asked the woman with surprise.

"A few days ago. We were living with neighbours, but… we thought we should come into the hospital," said Lyra.

Sayre peeled off her coat and held out her arm to reveal a nasty burn.

"We've got these all over us," she said, tired. She knew that they had no insurance and no credit card to pay for care, but what could they do to her that had not already been done? If they threw them in jail at least they would be fed.

The woman frowned with concern and began scribbling on her clipboard.

"Come with me," she said.

She made them disinfect their hands and she gave them all masks.

They were taken to a small office. The children waited outside. A woman in a suit and mask peered at them from a desk.

"Please, make yourself comfortable," she said. There were only two chairs. Sayre and one of the other adults sat down. Lyra lingered by the doorway, keeping an eye on the little ones.

"It seems you have suffered some hardship," began the woman, nodding sympathetically. "Before we get started on treatments, we will need to know a few things."

Sayre shifted in her seat uncomfortably.

"There are different… levels… of care possible at a hospital," began the woman. "For the Virus, we have a few options. Some have different costs associated with them. We are a business, you understand."

They looked at her, waiting for her to continue.

"We have a few drug options for treatment of symptoms, like a cough suppressant, and medication to help with the broken blood vessels in the face."

Sayre's whole face was red at this point; even her eyes were awfully bloodshot.

"We have oxygen therapy to reduce the damage to the lungs and respiratory system," continued the woman. "Of course, that one is quite expensive."

"I heard there was a cure," said Sayre quietly.

"There is immunization available, yes. But we only have a limited number of doses and it is reserved for… special cases."

Sayre felt the rumble deep in her chest. She tried to suppress it, but she could not. It erupted out of her in a coughing fit.

The woman at the desk leaned back with disdain in her

eyes behind her mask and face shield.

"Cough suppressant for sure, then," she said, making a note on her computer. "Do you have insurance, or will you be paying cash?"

"We don't have insurance," said Claudette, a note of panic in her voice.

"Mommy?" said one of the children, popping into the office.   "I'm hungry."

"Just wait ma chère," said Claudette. "We are just getting checked into the hospital."

"Actually, we are not checking into the hospital here," said the woman at the desk. "We are establishing your treatment payment plan."

"Look, my house just burned down," said Sayre, getting impatient. "I don't have money. I thought the hospital helped everyone."

"I don't actually work for the hospital," corrected the woman. "I represent Healtheris. We offer the lowest interest rate around on a special healthcare credit card. We will take care of your stay at the hospital, and you can pay us back at a reasonable interest rate. You're in luck; right now we have a pandemic special rate." She pushed a stack of paperwork toward them on the desk.

The baby started to wail.

"Shh, shh," said Claudette, pulling out her breast to feed him.

"If he's under one, his treatment will be fifty percent off," said the woman loudly, trying to talk over the baby's cries. Claudette stood up and walked to the door, trying to quiet the babe.

"What's going on? How long until we see the doctor?" said one of the other adults, sitting down in the chair vacated by Claudette.

"Hold on," said the woman. "Can everyone please get out their identification cards?"

They looked at one another. One person pulled out a battered old wallet.

"I think I have something in here, but I'm not sure,"

she said. She pulled out a tattered old birth certificate. "Is this what you're looking for?"

The woman at the desk laughed.

"Well that proves that you were born, doesn't it? But no, we unfortunately need some photo ID."

"I don't have anything but these clothes I'm wearing," said Sayre tiredly.

"Well that is a problem, isn't it?" said the woman. "You may have to get some ID before we can admit you to the hospital."

Sayre sighed with exasperation and leaned back in the chair. She was feeling faint with hunger.

"I can't even think about this right now," she whispered.

There was a long silence.

"Well I'll tell you what we can do," said the woman. "We do have a less expensive option. We received a donation to offset the cost… we can offer isolation treatment."

"What's that?"

"We would put you in a room together for two weeks. You would get a daily allowance of food."

"Like prison?" murmured Lyra from the doorway.

"Excuse me?" said the woman.

"No that sounds fine," said Sayre with relief.

"And we have some little extras like painkillers if you remember a pocket of money somewhere," said the woman with a knowing gaze, as though she suspected that they were hiding cash somewhere and just too cheap to pay for healthcare.

"Great," said Sayre, standing up. "Let's go."

"Hold on a minute," said the woman. She counted them up and took notes on her computer.

"You are a lucky little bunch," she said. "With all the children, you're great candidates for the program. We can fit you all together in one room, and the children count for the full amount. Not the baby though. Just fifty percent for him." She frowned, turning to the baby. Her eyes fell on Claudette's breast. She brightened. "But the milk will save on food cost though."

She pressed a button on her desk. The hospital employee with the clipboard returned.

"These ones will be on the virus relief program," said the Healtheris rep.

"Excellent. Right this way," said the woman with the clipboard. She led them out of the office and down to the check-in desk.

"You're lucky," she whispered. "We've had to send so many people away."

After a similarly onerous rigmarole at the front desk, they got checked in.

They were all tested for the virus and most of them were carriers. The doctor checking them over saw Sayre's burns.

"It says here you had a fire accident?" she said.

Sayre nodded.

"Well that's not covered in the grant program," said the doctor. She lowered her voice. "But here." She dug around in a cabinet and handed Sayre antiseptic and bandages. "Don't tell anyone."

A patient transporter led them down a dark hallway to room 207.

"Here you go. Food service has already happened today, but an orderly will bring your daily allotment tomorrow."

The survivors of Dummer Mobile Home Park walked into the small room.

"Wow! A bathroom! With water!" said Alexandra, popping out of a sub-room.

"Yes. Since you're a larger group, you get some comforts," said the transporter. "For your safety, we are locking you in this suite. Please do not try to leave before your isolation period is over. The orderly will be by tomorrow. Good night." He shut and locked the door before anyone could say anything.

"Mummy I'm hungry," said a little boy.

"We just have to wait," said Claudette.

The room had a bed and a chair. They took the thin mattress off the bed and lay it on the floor so more people could use it.

Everyone peeled off their winter clothes and took a turn using the toilet.

"Let's have a bath," said Claudette to distract the children.

They stripped down and piled into the small bath. Even Claudette and the other mother joined them. The bathroom was full of giggles and splashes. The hot water was a blissful relief from the cold winter winds that blew them here. They washed away their woes and the soot from the fire.

"Drink up," said Claudette, and the children gulped down water from the tap. It would have to tide them over until the orderly brought them food tomorrow. The children bedded down on the floor that night feeling soft and clean.

Over the next few days the Dummer folks relaxed on the floor as best they could. It was warm enough here and every day they each got a juice and milk box, a bagel with cream cheese, a peanut butter sandwich, and other sundry dried snacks like raisins, popcorn, nuts, and hard cookies wrapped in plastic. For all but Lyra, who had enjoyed the hospitality of the Androscoggin Free Zone, this was a luxurious vacation.

"America has the best healthcare in the world," said one of the adults. No one disagreed because they didn't know any different.

Sayre started to feel better. A hot steamy bath went a long way. The rumble deep in her chest did not go away, but her eyes returned to a more normal colour. They scrubbed all the clothing in the bath and hung it to dry by the radiator in the little room.

One day after another passed. Lyra spent night and day on her phone, consuming an endless stream of media bits. She sat against the wall with the device plugged in, shifting her position every once in a while when a limb would start to tingle and numb. She watched all manner of content, especially silly videos and news, and she caught up on what Joan Whiteduck was up to. It made the days go by bizarrely quickly. Lyra had noticed when they were walking into the city that everyone here spent their lives like this, more in the digital world than the embodied one. There was no window in their room, but the news said that it was one of the harshest winters in recent history. Lyra checked in on the Androscoggin Free Zone. She scrolled through their feed and saw that things seemed okay.

When two weeks were up, they begged to stay longer but they were not allowed. Although she was looking better, Sayre was still coughing an awful lot.

"She may have pneumonia, or something of that nature. But even if we offered a diagnosis, which we will not, then how would you pay for treatment? Pneumonia is not covered by the pandemic grant."

They were able to secure one more night in the hospital, resorting to using the baby for sympathy. Everyone showered one last time. Lyra searched up options online.

The Care Seminary was constructing free private hospitals all over the country, but there weren't any very close by. They would have to travel north on foot to Goreham. Lyra had always wanted to see the big city but it would be an awful trek for the children.

"We can't walk that far," said Claudette.

"It's up to you," said Sayre. "We can walk you back to Dummer if you like, on the way up."

It was a difficult decision. There was no telling what had happened in the shacks on Dirt Row in this past bitterly cold two weeks, and now they were quarantined and virus free. The hospital would not spare vaccines for them.

"You could always join the protesters outside," said

the nurse. "They have a soup kitchen that people are sponsoring, and they're even offering classes out there."

With tears and trepidation, they left the hospital and explored the tent city. The nurse was right; there was a food tent, and boxes of donated items were being prepared and distributed for the people wintering here.

These aren't protesters, thought Lyra, whose idea of protest was defined by Joan's acts of public defiance, not people with no other options.

The children were in good spirits, running up and down the rows of tents, making people smile as they passed, or grumble if they were trying to get through. The adults explained their situation to the volunteers in the food tent. If they stayed here, the volunteers could find them a tent to bunk into, and the children would even have access to a little day school. They decided to stay, for at least the winter. Sayre and Lyra decided to continue on to Goreham. Sayre could not sleep outside. The cold air made her cough so hard she could hardly breathe.

They hugged and kissed goodbye, wishing each other well.

"At least you're feeling better than before," said Lyra. "And we get to see Goreham."

"I've been there before, a long time ago," said Sayre. "It was only a quick visit but it was enough for me." Cities could be dangerous and Sayre had been in some danger or other her whole life. When she was younger, the dangers were different. She coughed hard and stumbled forward, grabbing her belly protectively. Now that she was older there were new kinds of struggles to contend with.

It turned into a strangely warm day and they slogged through slushy streets. As they turned up onto the highway for the long and windy stretch of their journey, Lyra noticed how tough her mother was. She had often thought her weak: weak for her addiction to cigarettes, weak for getting attached to no-good men, weak for wanting so little from life. Lyra felt hindsight shame tinge her cheeks red. Her mother was strong.

They walked and walked. The fortnight convalescence at the hospital had done them both well and they were in good spirits. Their feet would be blistered and sore, but if the weather held up they would reach the Care Centre at the outskirts of Goreham by evening.

The lights and smog of the city preceded it, as well as the buzz of drones. Lyra and Sayre felt the shift in energy as they got closer. They took an exit off the highway and soon they entered a more populated area. They encountered a giant fence crowned with security cameras and barbed wire, punctuated by marble pillars. They peered inside and saw massive palatial estate houses decorated with strings of sparkling electric lights for the holidays. The fence stretched out along the road for several kilometres. Almost every entry gate was guarded by a man with a visible semi-automatic assault weapon.

"I wonder who lives there?" said Lyra.

"You could fit all of Dummer Mobile Home Park in one of those," said Sayre.

It was strange that there was so much wealth in this country but it was in the hands of so few.

The estates gave way to a small suburban commercial district. In the distance, they saw the lights of a large institutional looking building. It was the new Care Centre.

When they finally arrived it was night. They approached the large entrance and found that here too, there were armed guards.

"I thought this hospital was free," said Lyra.

"It is. Patients are welcome. Just not the government," said the guard.

Lyra read online that there was a conflict growing between the Care Movement and the federal government. The last regime welcomed their help but this one felt threatened by their rapid expansion, and more troubling, their support from the public. Where there were no public offices or services anymore, there were Care Centres very visibly performing what other countries would consider public works, but what the United States of America left to the free market.

Lyra and Sayre went inside. There was a tent city in the front lobby. The place was full.

"Are you pregnant?" said a nurse coming toward them.

"Yes," said Sayre.

"Please come right this way," said the nurse.

They followed the nurse to an assessment area, where they were triaged to see a doctor quickly, due to Sayre's pregnancy.

"What is triage?" asked Lyra.

"It means we assess and order patient care based on urgency and need."

It was a system based on equity. Lyra was surprised. Her whole life it was all about who had the most money or power. She almost felt like they didn't deserve it, simply because she did not know about human rights and she had been enculturated not to value each life as an equal precious gift.

The doctor determined that Sayre was dangerously malnourished for a pregnancy, and she was put on a nutrient drip immediately.

"When your levels are more healthy, we'll immunize you for the virus," said the doctor. Vaccines were in short supply, but Lyra was given one due to her proximity to Sayre. She felt guilty thinking about Claudette, Alexandra and the others they had left behind.

"As you can see, we are over capacity," said the nurse, wheeling Sayre with her IV into a bathroom. "I'm so sorry but this is the only private space we have."

"I've never had private space," said Lyra. "Don't worry about it."

"If you're hungry, there is a cafeteria on the third

floor," said the nurse. "We appreciate donations, but you
are welcome to eat regardless."

"Thank you," said Sayre.

"I'll be back to check on you when I can." Then the
nurse left.

Lyra went down to the cafeteria to get some dinner
for her and her mother. There were metal tins lined up
under heating lamps with various stew-like dishes. She
regretted not being able to contribute to the donation jar.
She made up two plates and brought them upstairs.

In their little bathroom, Lyra saw a power outlet. She
plugged her phone into the wall and prepared for another
long stay. As her phone powered on, Lyra saw that she
had a message from Sikivu, the filmmaker she met in
Androscoggin Free Zone.

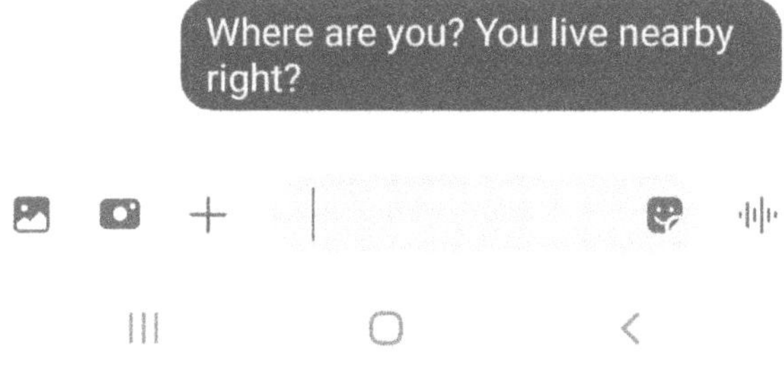

It was short and to the point. Lyra responded.

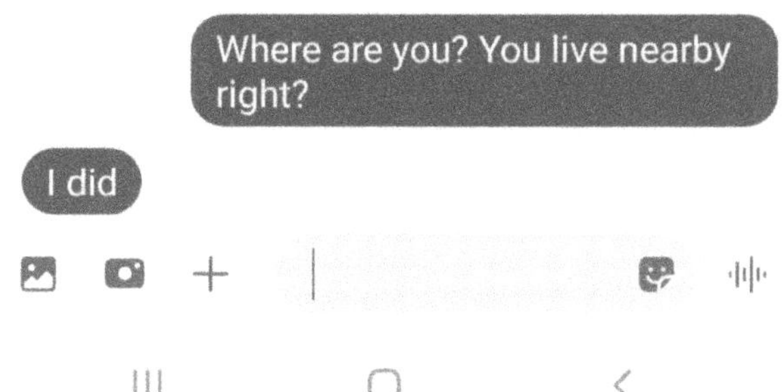

She hesitated to tell Sikivu about the fire. It would
only worry her and Lyra didn't particularly want to talk
about it. She missed Papa Gilles, and as she thought of
him she felt a pang of sadness and pushed the thoughts

away, focusing on the small blue glowing screen in front
of her eyes.

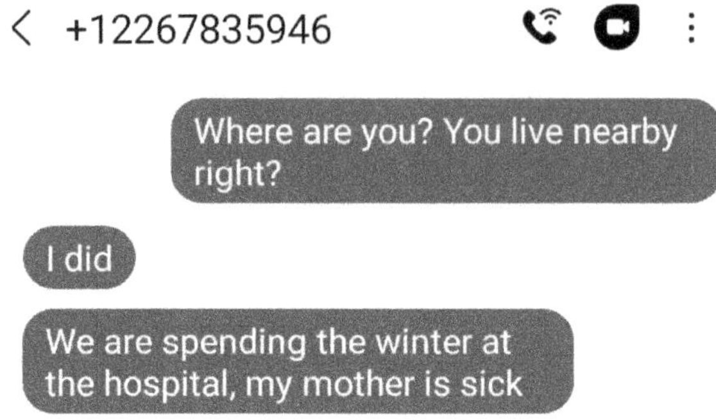

Suddenly Sikivu was online and messaging back.

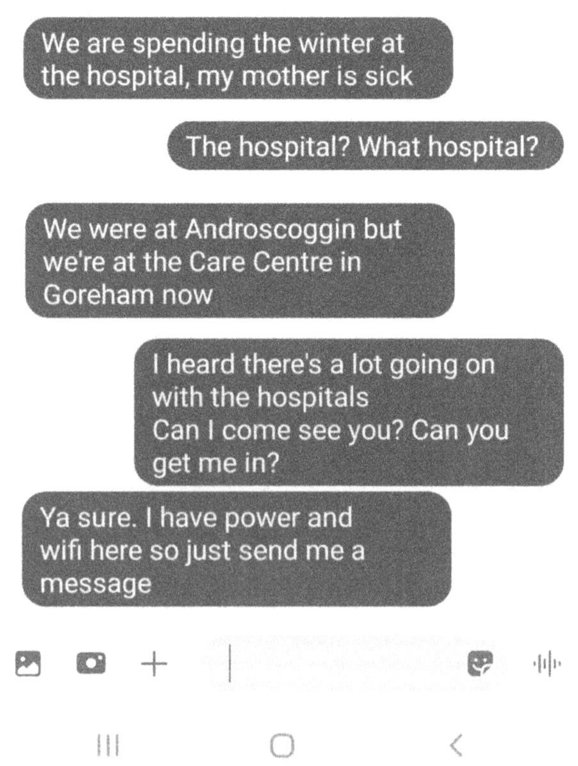

Lyra was enjoying these newfound luxuries.

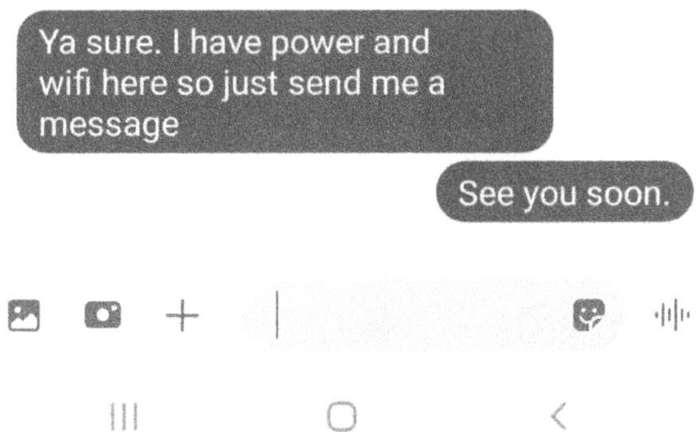

CHAPTER 9: Sikivu

Sikivu showed up at the Care Centre a few days later.

This building is brand new, she thought. She was mentally filing away these details as she documented everything with her camera. Her Androscoggin Free Zone piece was wrapping up and she was ready for the next project. She had never visited a Care Centre before, so Lyra Muse would provide the perfect entry point for the story. Care Centres were hot in the news right now. The government was describing the multi-level organization as a cult, and there were even whispers they circulated on questionable fringe media networks that it was a terrorist organization. They claimed that despite outwardly appearing to be a moral enterprise providing care to the needy, the wealthy higher-ups were planning a state takeover. It seemed far-fetched but Sikivu wanted to get the scoop directly from the source.

Lyra Muse met her at a side entrance just in case. Sikivu could see that the girl had grown leaps and bounds since the last time she had seen her only a few short months ago. She still had that serious expression.

"Follow me," said Lyra.

Sikivu followed. She was continuously rolling, stealthily capturing footage along the way. She had mastered the art of inconspicuously filming.

"Here it is," said Lyra, scooting into her mother's room.

"Wow, tight isn't it?" said Sikivu.

"There were eleven of us in a room at Androscoggin Hospital," said Lyra. "And we were lucky to get a room."

The situation is worse than I thought, thought Sikivu.

"This is my mother, Sayre," said Lyra.

"Nice to meet you."

"Hi," said Sayre.

"I met Lyra at the Androscoggin Free Zone," said Sikivu.

"Okay," said Sayre, nodding slowly.

Sikivu could see that either Sayre was uncomfortable or that she didn't know about that.

"When I… took Starlight on an adventure," said Lyra.

"Okay. Nice to meet you," said Sayre.

"I make little films," said Sikivu, "about what's going on in the world, things I find interesting."

"She's an artist," said Lyra.

Sayre looked at the woman standing by the bed. She was fairly well dressed, outfitted for the elements with a rucksack and good practical boots. Her hair was clean. She looked to be in her mid-twenties or so, but she could have been older if she had a comfortable upbringing.

Can I interview you?" asked Sikivu.

"What do you want to know?" said Sayre.

"Tell me everything."

Sikivu set up a popup tripod from her bag. She wished there were better light in here, but interviewing in a bathroom did give the video a certain valence of desperation.

Sayre told her about her childhood, the places she grew up. She skimmed a little in the middle, looking uncomfortably at Lyra. She talked about Dummer and having children. She talked about the fire and hot tears streamed down her face.

"Thank you," said Sikivu softly. "Please go ahead and take a minute."

Sayre waited calmly with her eyes shut, closing out thoughts of the fire, focusing on documenting the story, forcing herself not to feel too much until later.

"Then Lyra told us about the hospitals," said Sayre. "So we came here."

"That brings us to you." Sikivu turned to Lyra. "Can you tell us about what happened next?"

Lyra breathed a sigh of relief that Sikivu was not asking her about the fire. She couldn't talk about it. She talked about Androscoggin, the children, the tent city, the journey.

"What made you decide to take the journey when so many others did not?" asked Sikivu.

"I was worried about the baby," said Lyra. "When I saw my mother lying on the floor in the shacks, she looked half dead. The smell of burning made me sick. There was no life left there for us."

Sikivu looked at Lyra's serious expression. She decided to push.

"How do you feel about the criticism that people like you, without insurance, are profiting off the pandemic by leeching off the system?"

Lyra blinked her big eyes slowly and frowned.

"You can try and try all your life to do things yourself, like we did in Dummer Mobile Home Park," she said. "But when there's no school, and then there's no food, how do we get by when the sickness comes?" she said. "Why is there no place in this world for people who want to live simple? When mum and I came here we saw mansions big as a Megamart. Why do we have to live like that to get by? I just want to take a bath, and have enough to eat, and make my paints. That's all. Is there a place for us in this world? Or is there something wrong with me?"

Sikivu looked at Lyra through her lens.

"Good take," she said, referring to the film footage.

"I'm serious Sikivu," said Lyra. "Am I crazy?"

Sikivu thought for a moment. She realized that as smart as Lyra seemed, she was just a kid. This tiny sliver of culture was all she had ever known. She didn't have a formal education to give her insight into other ways of being either.

"There's a whole world out there, Lyra," she said. "There are all kinds of places and people living all sorts of different ways."

"You mean like Androscoggin Free Zone?"

"Sure, but even better than that. In the villages my great-grandparents come from in India, artists are seen as blessed, almost like saints."

Lyra thought about that.

"Or in Cape Breton, at the intentional community where my first big documentary was filmed, everybody takes care of everybody else. And in the country they live in, when you're sick you just go to the hospital and get treated. The politicians who run the country aren't millionaires, they're normal people. They use the public hospital too."

Lyra looked surprised. "So we don't have to live like this…"

Sikivu shook her head.

"So this is what America is now?"

"Well no," said Sikivu, taken aback. She wasn't quite ready to say that. "America is still the best, even after all this…" she trailed off, not sure who she was performing nationalism for.

"What would Joan say?" asked the girl.

"Joan? Joan Whiteduck?" said Sikivu with a laugh, remembering Lyra's fondness for the activist.

"Yea. What would Joan say?"

"I don't know," said Sikivu.

What would Joan Whiteduck say? she thought.

Sikivu pushed it out of her mind.

"Can I please stay with you for a few days?" she asked.

Lyra looked at her mother in the hospital bed.

"Of course," said Sayre.

They all spent the week doing very important work. Lyra started volunteering for the hospital. She showed her gratitude for the immunization she received by bringing trays of food to people with the sickness. After all, she had experience caring for people with the Rosie. Sikivu spent the next week creeping around the hospital, slyly gathering footage for her hospital documentary. Sayre rested her tired body, leveled out her nutrition counts, and grew a new little life inside her.

"Well hello there," said a cheerful voice.

Sikivu had been leaning against the wall texting. She stood up straight and looked at the man speaking to her. He wore a long black dress with a stiff white collar. There was a sparkling red eye embroidered on his breast. It was a Care Pastor.

"Hello," she said, caught off guard. In the city, it was conventional to leave someone alone while they were texting, off in the digital world.

"I've seen you a few times now, so I thought I'd be neighbourly and say hello!" he said.

Sikivu made a mental note to be less conspicuous.

"Well thank you," she said.

"What brings you to the Centre, my sister?" he asked.

"Just family illness."

"I see you are filming," he said with a gleam in his eye.

Sikivu, who was usually very keen at analyzing people, found this man difficult to read.

"I'm an artist," she said honestly. "I'm always

filming. This camera is like an extra limb on me."

The man laughed.

"That's a first," he said. "I'm Pastor Jim."

"Nice to meet you, Jim."

They chatted a little more and then Jim released her, mercifully. He made it clear that she was on his radar, though. Sikivu found that Care Pastors almost always had some variation of the same personality—manically cheerful, mildly patronizing, incredibly guarded.

It must be part of their training, she thought. She made a mental note to look into infiltrating a Care Seminary. She knew it would be difficult because Care Product™ armed their production facilities with the firepower of a small country, so the training of their management and missionary classes would probably have a similarly guarded scrutiny.

Sikivu was sufficiently spooked by her encounter with Pastor Jim that she spent the rest of the day in the small bathroom occupied by Lyra and Sayre, reviewing footage.

When Lyra was done her volunteering for the day, she returned to the room.

"Do you have a link to your work online?" asked Lyra. "I'd like to see it."

Sikivu sent her a private link to her documentary about Gray House and The Order. Lyra and Sayre watched it while Sikivu worked on editing.

"What did you think?" asked Sikivu when they were done.

"That's a cool place," said Lyra. "And they're the ones who started Femnonymous…"

Lyra had grown up her whole life without pronouns online, because back in the 2040s, a group called Femnonymous were the catalyst of a mass movement of hackers who engineered a gender-chaos algorithm that randomly changed he/she/they on the internet. Of course, some languages never had he/she to begin with, but those that did were changed forever online. To this day, the internet was still shifting gender pronouns constantly, to the chagrin of the hatemongers who held tight onto forcing heteronormative gendering onto other people. The movement was initiated by Sikivu's friend Artemis Elmahdy's mother, Mercury, one of the leaders of The Order and the Gray House community.

The next morning Lyra and Sikivu went down to the cafeteria for breakfast.

"Well hello there!"

Sikivu looked up to see Pastor Jim approaching.

"This must be Lyra," he said, smiling with a gleaming row of white teeth at the young teen.

Lyra frowned at him and said nothing.

"So I see you're a documentary filmmaker," he said, turning to Sikivu.

Pastor Jim's been doing his research, thought Sikivu.

"Yes, I'm an artist, as I said."

"I watched 'Gray House'. You're pretty critical of America, aren't you?"

Sikivu sighed with exasperation. This was a critique she often got, and was the subject of most of her hate mail.

"I make documentaries about the real issues we need to face in America. But America is still great." Her smile was wide without a trace of irony. Pastor Jim heard the sincerity in her voice.

"I see," he said.

"Isn't that what you're doing here too? People say the Care Movement hates America because you're building these Care Centres for healthcare and education instead of relying on the government to do it… but isn't what you're really doing providing care for Americans who need it?"

Pastor Jim looked at her with his mastered impassive expression.

"Mercury Elmahdy is considered a terrorist. You glorify her in this documentary," he said.

"I've heard the Care Movement called a terrorist organization. It's all about perspective," she said, dropping her voice at the word 'terrorist'. She had noticed cameras everywhere in this place. She was sure that there was no privacy here.

"Do you think that's true?"

"I'm a storyteller, not a judge and jury," said Sikivu.

"Would a terrorist organization allow you to be here?"

"Probably not."

"We are going to let you stay. Please don't wear out our hospitality."

"We?" said Sikivu. "Is that a 'royal we', or are there others watching me?"

"You, better than anyone, should know there are always others watching."

Sikivu found it difficult to decide how she felt about the Care Movement. They opened all these free hospitals, seemingly with no strings attached. She had noticed downstairs that they were soon unveiling a school wing. The Care Movement was like a mini-government providing the social services the state did not. She understood why the state felt threatened. The existence of Care Centres was an unintentional criticism of the state. It reminded her of the Fall of Rome when a fringe organization from the Middle East later called Christianity started doing something similar. They were persecuted, and called the equivalent of radicals and terrorists, but in the Dark Ages, their abbeys and churches were all that was left of the socialist state. The Catholic Church and its descendants eventually created a global empire.

"What's the Care Movement's plan?" asked Sikivu. "What's the end game?"

"There is no end game," said Pastor Jim. "We just Care™."

Sikivu did not doubt that Pastor Jim believed that. But the Care Movement was a large organization with many levels of governance. Who knew what they were talking about in the upper tiers of the enclave.

"Well thank you for your hospitality," said Sikivu.

That night there was a massive storm, and the weather took a turn for the worst. The temperature plunged down, even though days before the snow had completely melted and it felt like spring. Weather systems over the last fifty years or so had shifted erratically and it was hard to predict nowadays.

People flooded into the Centre. Many homes were simply not equipped to deal with intense weather conditions, and extreme cold in particular. Sikivu was shocked to see so many people without shelter. She had grown up in a gated community without hardship. She always attended good schools, and she never went without medical care. Part of her struggled not to judge these parents for not providing better for their children. She could hardly understand their dilemma.

"You should see where I grew up," said Lyra quietly.

Sikivu looked at Lyra, a mere thirteen year old girl who was grown up.

When I was thirteen I was reading mystery novels and thinking about when I would get boobs, thought Sikivu.

The next day Sikivu crept out of the hospital to find Lyra some textbooks. She was anxious about not being able to get back in, but it was important to try. She looked up the nearest public school and the route to get there. She knew that public transport was a dangerous transmission zone for the Rosie, but she had health insurance from her parents so she wasn't very worried. She put on her mask and made her way to the station. When she got there, she found that all the buses were cancelled, and indeed had been decommissioned long ago. There was one train that would take her part of the way. She waited with the others, mostly other women of colour, and then climbed aboard when it arrived.

The inside of the train was covered with graffiti and falling apart.

"Is this the right train?" she asked a woman beside her. The other woman looked her up and down.

"What, not fancy enough for you?" she said with a snort.

"No, I… it's just… I'm surprised is all. I'm not from around here."

"The City sold the trains to Oil Corp and they keep putting up the price but the trains are falling apart," said someone close by.

"I see."

Sikivu disembarked at her stop and walked the rest of the way to the school.

"I'm looking for textbooks for a thirteen year old," she said to the secretary at the front desk.

"Is she registered here?" said the secretary with a yawn.

"Ummm… sort of," said Sikivu. She stood up taller in a more authoritative stance and slipped cash onto the desk. The secretary took her money and gave her books, no questions asked.

Sikivu made her way back to the Care Centre. She texted Lyra to let her back in, and they pulled it off with no problems, even though there was now a growing tent city here at the Care Centre too.

"Here," she said, handing Lyra the books. "Check these out."

Lyra took the books and saw they were for school.
"Thanks."

"Maybe we can go down to the cafeteria later and talk about it," said Sikivu.
"Sure."

It turned out that the books were sponsored by a variety of corporations. The history book talked mostly about the history of their companies and how they were the glue holding America together.

"I think I would have been better off getting you a

fantasy novel," said Sikivu. "This is just… bizarre."

"There's no mention of indigenous people in this history book," said Lyra, confused.

"To be fair, even at the charter school I went to we didn't learn much about the actual history of this place. You probably know more than I do just from listening to Joan."

Like other public works, education was defunded to pay for border control and military operations to quash the secession movements. Corporations filling the gaps through sponsorships took it upon themselves to re-write their own company's self-importance into the textbooks.

Next Sikivu decided she would try to help Sayre find a place to live after the baby was born. She searched online for apartments and jobs close by that Sayre could do. She found that there were lots of jobs, but none of them would pay for a decent apartment.

"This can't be right," she mumbled, running the numbers. It didn't make any sense. Sikivu took Lyra to visit a few potential places. As they looked room to room at smashed windows, dingy fingerprinted walls, dripping rusty pipes and peeling wallpaper, Sikivu realized that living in the bathroom at the Care Centre was actually much better. She couldn't imagine raising a baby there, but doing it in one of these dives was worse. Eventually she gave up on that too. She thought of the parties she'd attended in gated communities where tables piled high with food went to waste in vast rooms no one lived in. No amount of well-meaning effort on behalf of one little family was going to change the system that needed to be dismantled to help not only Lyra and Sayre, but everyone else too.

Weeks passed and Sayre's belly grew. Sikivu gathered enough footage of the hardships and triumphs around her to make another documentary. Lyra got lost in a digital fog with her newfound constant access to the internet.

The days grew warmer, and soon enough, spring was

upon them. Finally it was time for Sayre to deliver the baby. She arrived in the pale yellow light of morning after hours of labour. Sikivu documented the baby's first moments of life on earth, and decided to end her documentary with new life and hope. She had a feeling deep inside as she filmed the little family's smiles of joy that her time here was over. She had done what she could for them, and they for her, and now she would be on her way. They said their goodbyes and parted ways, and Sikivu went back to New York City.

CHAPTER 10: Sayre

Sayre lay in the hospital bed looking into the eyes of her little one. She was a calm and quiet baby, not a screamer like Lyra. Despite her difficulties getting to this world, she seemed to be in good health. The nurse warned her that they would need to stay another week or more to be monitored, because the rate of infant cancer, particularly in large cities, had skyrocketed in the last few generations and now they automatically checked for signs and symptoms before discharging. Pastor Jim gently reminded them that now that the baby was born and they were mostly recovered from their winter ordeal, they would have to leave the Centre to make room for other patients.

Sayre was avoiding the thought of leaving. It was hard enough knowing there was nothing left for them in the home they once knew, but now they were in Goreham with a baby. Everything was harder with a baby. Where would they go next? A rumble started deep in her chest, and grew into a fit of uncontrollable coughing. It was so bad she had to put down the baby. She hacked up a large gob of mucus into a piece of toilet paper. She breathed for a moment, waiting out the chest pain.

"Sorry little one," she cooed at last, picking the baby back up into her arms. "Mommy is okay now." Sayre had been experiencing this for years. It hadn't flared up in a few months because she didn't have access to cigarettes here.

She tossed the toilet paper into the garbage. *Maybe I'll quit,* she thought.

Lyra came into the room with a tray of food from the cafeteria.

"Here mom," she said. She laid the tray across Sayre's legs and held out her arms to take the baby.

Sayre smiled with relief and handed her over.

"Such a good big sister," she said.

Lyra beamed and kissed the baby gently on the forehead.

"Have you decided what to name her yet?" asked Lyra.

Sayre was waiting for the final discharge from the doctor to name the child. In the Tanakh, the most sacred book of the Jewish people, they waited eight days to name a baby because infant mortality was common. Life began at eight days. Until then, the baby was like a limb of Sayre herself, at the mercy of her mother's care. Sayre did not call herself Jewish, but she had a grandmother long ago who told her a few things before they were separated.

"Not yet," she said to Lyra. As she said it, the name appeared in her mind like a flash of light. *Sudbina*. It was her grandmother's name. It meant 'destiny' in Croatian, from Sanskrit.

She would tell Lyra on the eighth day.

The day they were discharged was bright and sunny. The air smelled of spring.

"Perfect for a long walk," said Lyra with a deadpan

expression, although she meant to be funny.

"I'm getting too old for this," groaned Sayre, wrapping up the baby in a fabric sling to carry her under her coat. They had one last meal at the cafeteria for breakfast. Lyra filled her bag with items that would last longer. She hated stealing from the Care Centre but Sayre would need some sustenance for the baby's milk.

They walked the highway in the brisk spring air. It was a much easier journey than it had been on the way north.

"We could try Randolph," said Lyra. "Papa Gilles' cabin wouldn't do for one of these cold winters, but we could spend the summer there for sure. And maybe the Care Centre could let us back next winter."

"Sounds like a good idea." Sayre was exhausted already from walking and she couldn't think. Lyra's plan was as good as any, and Sayre had trouble making decisions her whole life.

"You could get pregnant again, so we have a reason to go back to the Care Centre," said Lyra cheekily.

Sayre laughed. The hacking cough tore out of her.

"Let me take a turn with Sudbina." Lyra took the baby.

"It sounds so easy," said Sayre at last. "Getting pregnant is the easy part. It's giving birth you have to watch out for. I feel like I've been shipwrecked."

"We'll be okay," said Lyra. They walked on in silence for a moment.

"Mom, what's with your cough? Are you okay?"

"I'm fine."

"You haven't been smoking, have you?"

"No... It's just working its way out of my system I guess."

They turned off the highway at the route to Dummer Mobile Home Park. Sayre wanted to say hello to familiar faces. Lyra felt ashamed about it, but she didn't want to see anyone. She couldn't bear the thought of ever seeing their burned up trailer again. She went on to Inas' instead.

"Now that you've had your vaccine, you spend the night on Dirt Row," said Lyra. "I'll be with Inas, and I'll come get you tomorrow morning and we'll go to Randolph."

Sayre walked down the stretch of road into the park with Sudbina tied to her chest. It was muddy so she had to weave around potholes and soft earth so she wouldn't soak her ragged boots.

It was eerie walking into camp, where frames of twisted metal remained like skeletons. Some folks stretched tarps and boards over half-burned trailers, salvaging what was left and moving back in. Others were burned beyond recognition. The snow was gone and the events of early winter were laid bare.
Suddenly she realized that the ruins in front of her were her home. She stood there in a trance, lost in painful memory and indescribable feeling. It looked so small and inconsequential, but that was where she had raised her children. The corners of her eyes stung but she could not cry. She felt like if she started she would never stop. She was not a very sentimental person, having learned to go numb to things long ago, but she could not tear her eyes away.

Suddenly Sudbina let out a sharp cry. It was uncharacteristic of her. Sayre's trance broke and she looked at the little face tucked away in her jacket.

"Lunch time?" she murmured, licking her finger and rubbing the baby's little tongue. She walked to the 'playground' area. Wooden bench seats and plastic pegs and fixtures had not survived the fire, but the metal monkey bars were intact. Sayre leaned up against them and pulled out her breast to feed the baby.

"Life goes on," she said.

Sayre went to Dirt Row to see who was still here. People looked at her with surprise bordering on shock.

Folks rarely left Dummer Mobile Home Park, and if they did they never came back. The last time they saw her she was sick and skinny, and now the warmth in her cheeks was healthy and her baby looked fine.

"You're looking good Sayre," said Old Jean with a cackle. She could see he'd lost more teeth this winter.

"Don't come too close," said an old neighbour. "I haven't kicked the Rosie yet. We keep getting it here." Sayre could see that less than half of them were wearing masks.

"It's okay Annette, I got a vaccine," she said. "The baby's got one too. We're fine."

"Shouldn't-a done that," said Jean. "Vaccine'll giver autism!"

"Where's your medical degree, eh Jean?" said Sayre.

"Don't need one, I got common sense. Those degrees ain't real anyway. It's all a bunch of communist propaganda in them schools and hospitals anyways."

"We went to a Care Centre," said Sayre. She knew Old Jean took pills from Pastor Ned.

"Pah," he said, spitting on the ground.

Sayre didn't mind the banter. In fact, she almost missed it. These people had their quirks, but they were her people. Despite the hardships, she would rather be here than up in Goreham in a scary apartment with a bunch of heroine addicts. Here they just smoked bad weed and thought vaccines gave you autism.

"Did Claudette come back?" asked Sayre.

"Haven't seen her."

Sayre spent the night in one of the shackies on Dirt Row. These days, they were one of the better places to be. Now that spring was here, things were waking up and folks were rebuilding. Soon enough the whole town would be like Dirt Row, a mishmash of found materials assembled into shelters.

When Lyra showed up to get her with Starlight and her bicycle in tow, she had second thoughts about leaving.

"I don't know if we should go somewhere else, Lyra," she began.

"What, you mean you want to stay here?" Lyra's voice held a touch of disdain.

"Living in a fancy hospital's got you on a high horse, I see," snapped Sayre. Then she softened. She remembered the fire and brimstone she felt at that age.

No use arguing with a teenager, she thought.

"Sweetheart, it's a dangerous world out there. We have people here looking out for us. That means everything… trust me, I know."

"I can't stay here," said Lyra, lowering her voice and gesturing around the park.

Sayre looked around, trying to see it through her daughter's eyes. The burned ruins, the tarps and charred wood, the muddy road. It looked like broken dreams. She sighed.

"We have a baby now. I can't just go wandering off into the unknown. We need to provide for this baby."

"Do you really want to raise her here?"

"I raised you here, and you're fine."

A tear burned the corner of Lyra's eye. She blinked it away quickly.

"We don't even have a home mom."

Sayre was silent. It was true.

Who's going to build us a home? I have this baby to take care of.

"Brandon will come back and help us."

"Bullshit!" shouted Lyra. "Brandon's never helped anyone with anything!"

"Lyra!" scolded Sayre. That was all she could say. Then she erupted in a coughing fit.

When she got her coughing under control, she was torn. If they stayed here then she would have to go find a client. With the baby it would be difficult. She groaned inwardly. Old Jean would take them in, but at a cost that Sayre didn't think she could stomach.

"I'm leaving," said Lyra quietly. She turned around and left.

"Lyra! Wait! Come back here!" said Sayre. She couldn't bear to lose Lyra right now.

Lyra paused and turned around, waiting. Sayre looked at her and imagined Gilles' cabin.

Even though he's gone, he's still taking care of us, thought Sayre.

"Fine, I'm coming," she said, and she started walking.

Sayre's feet ached from hours on the road. She hadn't had this much exercise since before the baby was born. Still, it felt glorious to be out of the hospital. The spring sun cast a hopeful primrose light. Starlight ran back and forth along the road, barking happily. The dog enjoyed her time with Inas but she was glad to be back with Lyra. She was obsessed with the baby, sniffing her and wagging her tail, running off and running back again.

When they were approaching the turn off the highway, Starlight already knew the way. She took off down the dirt road.

"It's okay, that's where we're going," said Lyra.

It felt like forever going down that road. Sayre was completely exhausted and Lyra was unsure of where to go. Thankfully Starlight knew and popped out of the bushes near the overgrown laneway.

"Almost there now," said Lyra.

They followed the old trail up into the bush, and there was the cabin. Sayre dragged her feet after Lyra up to the door. The wood stairs had long since turned to dust but there was an old washtub turned over to climb up onto. Lyra opened the door and they walked inside. She called Starlight in and shut the door. She seemed anxious to get the dog inside.

Oh yes, this was where they found the dog... dogs, thought Sayre.

She looked around the room inside the cabin. It

was beautiful. Everything was covered with a fine layer of dust, but she could deal with that first thing in the morning. She hobbled over to the horsehair couch and plopped down on it. Like clockwork, the baby started sniffling.

"Such a good girl," cooed Sayre. "She waited until we got here to ask for food, did you see that?"

Lyra nodded. She was looking at her mother and looking around the room. She seemed anxious.

"What is it?" asked Sayre.

"Do you like it?"

"It's beautiful, Lyra."

I don't know what we'll eat, but sure it's beautiful, thought Sayre. *You'll learn to adapt as I have, little one.* She touched the baby's soft cheek tenderly.

Lyra gave her a rare little smile. She went over to the beds and pulled off the sheets to shake out the dust. When she came back, Sayre was nursing Sudbina.

The sun went down quickly and soon it was pitch black inside the cabin. They went to bed snug under the sheets feeling the deep peace of coming home for the first time in a long time.

Sayre woke up to the sound of forest birds. She had woken up in a lot of strange places, but never to the sound of birds before. Her body sunk into the middle of the old mattress like a hug. She understood why Lyra wanted to come here.

Sudbina lay between her breasts sleeping soundly. Her little lips quivered with breath as her chest rose and fell. Sayre wanted to stroke her soft head, but she didn't want to touch her for fear she would wake.

Best not disturb her, she thought.

Instead she looked around the room, taking in her surroundings. It was basic, but comfortable, with a camp kitchen and even a table to sit at. She laid in bed for another hour, half sleeping, resting comfortably in the bed. Very faintly, she could smell Gilles in the bedsheets. Here in the stillness of the cabin, it was a pleasant reminder, not a painful one.

I hope his spirit is here, she thought.

Eventually Lyra woke too. She got up, stretching her arms out.

"I'll be back," she said, grabbing their water bottles and a bucket.

When she returned, she had water.

"Where did that come from?" asked Sayre.

Lyra just smiled a tiny smile.

"Here," she said, holding out a water bottle.

Sayre took it and drank. It was ice cold, and tasted sweet.

"Is it safe to drink?" she asked.

"Of course!" said Lyra, and then her face faltered.

"Lyra, are you sure?"

"Papa Gilles drank this water all his life," said Lyra indignantly. "But Joan said they were planning to poison it. I don't know if they did yet or what."

Sayre ran it back and forth over her tongue. Then she shrugged.

"Can't be worse than that sludge we were drinking at the hospital."

The water in Goreham was brownish because there were major problems with the water infrastructure. The government hadn't updated it since pipes were installed in the late 1700s in some places. Instead of fixing the pipes they just pumped the system with chemicals. The result was a strange cocktail that authorities insisted was safe to drink. This water tasted much better.

Sudbina opened her eyes. She was hungry.

"Time to get up," laughed Sayre, sitting up in bed.

Lyra rummaged in the dresser and then brought something over. She wiped it off with the corner of her shirt and then held it out for Sudbina.

It was a small, smooth silver bird. It had a handle for a tiny hand to hold it. Sudbina held it instantly to her mouth. The bird's fat little body was too big to choke on. Lyra and Sayre both laughed.

"There's more toys in the dresser," said Lyra. She ran back over and picked up a few things.

Sayre looked up. Her eldest daughter paused on her way back over, looking down at a tiny doll in her hands. She smoothed down its dress and straightened its hair.

"Too small for Sudbina," said Lyra quietly.

"I guess it's yours then," said Sayre. As soon as the words came out she regretted them. She didn't want to insult Lyra, who was getting too old for dolls.

Lyra was silent. She'd never had a doll before. She didn't really know what to do with it, but she liked its friendly face. She wondered if one of Papa Gilles' sisters had loved this doll. She slipped it into a special little pocket in her satchel with her paint brushes.

Sayre got out of bed. She investigated the kitchen. There was a real cast iron cookstove. If they ever found food, they would be able to cook here. Sayre looked inside. Everything appeared to be in working order.

"Papa Gilles told me not to light this up without clearing out the nests in the chimney," said Lyra.

"Do you know how to do that?"

"Yes, he showed me."

"All right, let's start there."

Sayre sat out front holding Sudbina while Lyra leaned the old ladder on the mossy walls of the cabin. She scrambled up and onto the tin roof.

"Be careful," called Sayre.

Lyra reached in and found only a few handfuls of leaves built up inside. It took her just a few minutes to clear the pipe this time.

Soon they had a merry fire crackling in the stove. Sayre got water boiling. She was going to clean every inch of this place. She remembered the old washtub outside.

We'll clean the sheets another day, she thought. She would have at least one more night with the sheets that smelled of Gilles.

Lyra pulled all the food items out of her bag and put

them in the cupboard.

Sayre looked them over.

"Well it's enough for a few days at least," she said.

Lyra nodded. She looked like she wanted to say something but didn't.

"What?" said Sayre. "What is it?"

"There's a fishing hole nearby," said Lyra. "I never fished but I watched Papa Gilles do it. I could give it a try."

There was more that Lyra wasn't saying but Sayre didn't press.

"How far is the town where you got the flour?" said Sayre.

"Not too far."

Sayre considered. Maybe when she was feeling more recovered from childbirth she could find some clients there to help them out. Maybe they could find a nice family to clean house for, but more likely than not that would be difficult. She was willing to do what she had to to help out her family. For the first time, she considered the idea of staying here, but they would have to figure something out to make it work.

Lyra rooted around and found some fishing line and hooks. There was no rod, but she could try to make one with a branch. She set to work.

"Can you go by yourself or should I come with you?" asked Sayre.

Lyra was silent a moment. She was thinking about the last time she was at the fishing hole when she had nearly drowned. Best to have a sensible second opinion.

"Come with me."

Sayre wrapped up Sudbina and they set out to the fishing hole. Starlight led the way. She knew exactly where they were going.

When they arrived, Lyra showed Sayre around.

"Here is where the cooking fire is," she said, pointing to the crèche in the rocky outcropping. Sayre set to work gathering wood.

Lyra thought a moment and then rooted around beneath the mossy stones. She picked out a few worms and then turned the stones back over. She held up a wriggling worm and grimaced, unsure of how to get it on the hook.

"Bring it here," said Sayre.

Lyra brought over the hook and the worm. Sayre pushed it onto the hook from tip to tip and handed it back.

Lyra held the pole out over the hole as Papa Gilles had done. She tossed the baited line out into the water.

It wasn't long before she felt the bites. A few times she pulled the line up too soon, sure that there was a fish on the end but the line was bare. Eventually though, one yanked the line so hard it almost pulled her in. She hauled up the line, dragging the flopping fish out of the water. She wished she had more grace with the pole but she would need practice. The fish looked at her with panicked eyes, gasping heavily.

Lyra held the squirming fish in her hands. It was harder than it looked. She pulled Papa Gilles' bone-handled knife out of her bag. She steadied herself and sawed off its head. It was messy and sloppy, and the fish wriggled away from her a few times. She felt heartsick torturing the poor thing, but she did her best. It was better than letting it suffocate. Next time would be cleaner. Papa Gilles had poked a wire through the lips of his catches on a long line, but Lyra didn't have one. She brought the decapitated fish to Sayre and returned to the fishing hole.

By the afternoon they had a sizeable pile of fish. Sayre poked two onto sticks to roast over the fire. The rest they would bring back to the cabin to fry up for dinner and to smoke. Lyra took a break and they sat on rocks to eat their fish. Sayre pulled the skin off of hers. She knew it was healthy but she couldn't stomach it. Lyra crunched hers up along with Sayre's, the juicy fish oils dripping down her chin.

"I hope Sudbina likes fish as much as you do," said Sayre. Her milk would be tasting fishy for the foreseeable future.

Lyra caught a few more fish and then they packed them up in the bucket and headed back to the cabin. On the way they saw a grassy field.

"Let's stop here a minute," said Sayre.

They dipped off the road into the field. It was a rocky clearing with a few trees but mostly grass. Sayre told Lyra to pick a few handfuls.

"We can make a broom to sweep the house," she said.

Lyra scampered around gathering long grass.

"Doesn't mean we're going to stay," said Sayre. She didn't want to get Lyra's hopes up, even though things were looking better and better around here.

Back at the cabin Lyra took Sudbina while Sayre prepared the fish for smoking and frying. Over the next few days they settled into a comfortable flow in the space together. Lyra showed her mother where the brook was.

"I wonder if that dries up in the fall," said Sayre. "Between that drying up and snow could be a dangerous time without water."

"We could get a rain barrel," said Lyra.

Sayre considered. That was a precious and useful item, but potentially they could find one somewhere. If there was a dump nearby they could find a lot of things they might need. Sayre realized that Lyra was looking at her closely.

"I want to try to make it work for us," said Sayre. "I just worry about being so far from other people."

"I don't want to be around other people," said Lyra.

"Oh sweetie I know."

"Let's take a trip into Randolph," said Lyra. "Papa and I traded fish for those things we brought back with us last time."

Sayre brightened at the thought of visiting the town.

She wanted to know that if winter was harsh they could beg their way into somewhere not too far away.

"Alright," she said.

"We took filleted fish. I think they would appreciate smoked fish too."

Sayre and Lyra got to work catching and preparing enough fish to make a trip into town. By this time Sayre had resigned herself to the taste of fish, but she was excited to see what other possibilities were out there. Lyra described the General Store so beautifully.

"If they have seeds, maybe we can start a little garden?" said Lyra.

"Baby steps," said Sayre.

They wrapped up Sudbina and Lyra packed up the fish. Lyra looked worried.

"What is it?" asked Sayre.

"Nothing."

"Come on, I know you. Just tell me."

"It's Starlight," said Lyra. "This was where we found her, running away. I don't want to keep her locked inside but I don't want her to leave us."

"Starlight!" said Sayre sharply. The dog jumped up to attention. Sayre looked her in the eyes. She bent down. Starlight came over and sniffed the baby. Sudbina put out her little hand and stroked the dog's fearsome muzzle. Sayre scratched her behind the ears.

"I think we'll be okay," she said. "We can't leave her locked in here, she might tear the place apart trying to get out."

"Okay," said Lyra with hesitation in her voice.

They set off for Randolph. Lyra was right; the General Store was tidy and well-kept, just like the rest of the little town. The eaves were freshly painted white with a floral pattern painted on the side of the building. They went inside.

"Hello there," said the woman at the counter cheerfully. She was a little younger than Sayre but not much, with long braided hair. Her clothes were clean and well mended and she was leaning back in her chair with her socked feet up on the counter, reading a book. She brought her feet down as they came in.

"Oh please, stay comfortable," said Sayre. She and Lyra walked up to the counter.

"Back with more fish I see," said the woman.

"You remember me," said Lyra quietly.

"You came to see Joan Whiteduck, right?"

"Sort of. Well, yes I guess," said Lyra.

The woman leaned over the counter and looked into the bucket. There were whole fish there, and smoked fillets.

"Those will be easy to get rid of. A few people commented on your great filleting skills."

Lyra gulped.

"These aren't," she said honestly. "Papa Gilles… he…" she searched for the polite term. "He passed away," she said quietly.

"I'm sorry to hear that."

Lyra put the bucket up on the counter.

"I'm afraid I can't fillet yet," said Lyra.

"Not to worry," said the woman. "I can do it."

"I can help," said Sayre. "Though I'm nothing like Gilles."

The women prepared the fish and chatted.

"I'm Marie," said the Randolph General Store proprietor. She packed the fillets in brown paper and took them to the fridge.

Sayre dissolved into her hacking cough. Marie looked concerned.

"Don't worry, we've all been immunized," she said. "It's my cigarette lungs."

"That sounds serious," said Marie. "You should see a doctor."

"We spent the winter in the hospital," said Sayre. "We're doing better than before, trust me."

Marie still looked concerned but said nothing.

They spent far longer than necessary looking through all the beautiful items in the store. They picked a few things to trade for the fish. Sayre eyed a few items she would aim to find items to trade for in the future.

Maybe Lyra and I can make some brooms, she thought. Her homemade grass broom was working out well.

"Is there someone in town who can sharpen an axe?" she asked. The rusty old axe at the cabin was good enough for their rough broom, but it would need to be sharper to make something worth trading.

"I can," said Marie. "I'm a tinsmith so my tools need to be very sharp." She gestured to the beautiful tin items hanging from the ceiling.

"You made Lyra's candle holder," said Sayre with surprise.

"That's right," laughed Marie.

Sayre was impressed.

"What's this town like?" asked Sayre.

"It's a nice place. Quiet. Some might say boring. Folks are nice," said Marie.

Sayre nodded.

They said goodbye to Marie and headed back up to the cabin.

"She was nice," said Sayre.

Lyra nodded.

Over the next few days Lyra explored the woods around the cabin and Sayre contemplated what it would take to stay.

The walls would need to be insulated for winter, she thought. When Papa Gilles was a boy it probably didn't get cold enough to freeze them to death very often. Nowadays the weather was quite unpredictable, with flash freeze storms and flash melts. She also felt she would be quite lonely trapped inside. Spending last winter in the hospital bathroom without windows was hard on her. She would ask Lyra to find a big log they could roll over to sit on outside. If there were a place outside that was a bit more comfortable to sit it would be nice.

Don't get too attached, thought Sayre. It was a trauma-induced response she had developed over the years. When she got too relaxed, too comfortable, her hormones would shoot panic endorphins. She was in a constant state of fight or flight.

It was Lyra's birthday soon. Sayre wasn't sure what day it was but she knew that when the trees began to blossom it marked the day of her first daughter's birth. She made an excuse to Lyra and left her to take care of Sudbina and went into Randolph.

"Nice to see you again," said Marie with a grin at the General Store.

"You too," said Sayre. They chatted. Sayre felt awkward. She had never really had friends before and didn't know how to talk to other women. The women at Dummer Mobile Home Park treated her with a guarded suspicion because she had two – now three—children with different men, and she didn't seem to mind if those men were married or not. It was a lonely life. Marie made her feel right at home though. She usually didn't trust people, but she found herself telling Marie about Dummer, her family, the cabin.

"So what can I do for you?" asked Marie.

"It's my daughter's birthday," she said. "So I need to make a cake."

"That's so nice!" said Marie. "I have everything, for sure."

Sayre traded a grass broom for the ingredients.

"This is great handiwork," said Marie, inspecting the broom. "Of course, you need a sharper axe, but you mentioned that already," she said.

"I forgot to bring the axe," laughed Sayre.

"That's okay. Come visit me again some time," said Marie with a warm smile. She grabbed something from a bin.

"Take this jute twine too," she said. "I'm commissioning you to make some more of these brooms."

Sayre looked at the string, hesitant to take it. People rarely gave her something for nothing.

Marie nodded with encouragement. Sayre reached out and took the twine.

"Thank you," she said.

As she walked home with her cake parcel and the string dangling down, she felt it was a lifeline.

When Sayre came home she took the baby and sent Lyra outside. She made a nice little cake for Lyra's birthday. She baked it in the hot wood fired oven. It turned out heavy with butter, but delicious with a crispy top.

When Lyra came in from rambling outside, Sayre sang her happy birthday. Love glowed in all their eyes and they ate homemade cake that night.

"Fourteen," said Sayre, "I can hardly believe it." The last fourteen years flew by. There were ups and downs, but things finally seemed like they were going to be okay.

"Thank you mum," said Lyra.

The stove was still piping hot, so they boiled up buckets of water and filled the old washtub. All three took turns having a warm bath. Lyra got to go first because it was her birthday.

"It's pretty great here, isn't it mum," said Lyra.

"Yes," laughed Sayre. "It's pretty great."

They explored the woods and went for long walks along the roads, seeing where they led. No one lived close to them at all, but there seemed to be some properties that might get occasional visitors. They were careful to keep Starlight close by when they walked by those.

Sayre's cough did not go away. In fact, most nights she woke herself from coughing. She stuffed her pillowcase with grass under the pillow to let her sit up higher. She drank the old tea in an enamelware cup. It helped but her cough was persistent.

"I haven't smoked in months, I don't know where this is coming from," she said. "I must be getting old."

One day Sayre woke up choking. She could hardly breathe. Lyra was squeezing her hand beside the bed yelling at her to wake up. She sat up straight and coughed until the fit passed. Her entire chest was on fire and her mouth tasted like blood.

"We need to get you to a hospital," said Lyra.

"No!" said Sayre firmly. "You remember last time, we don't have any money. It would be a waste of time. I'd rather be here."

During their next visit to Randolph General Store, Lyra told on Sayre to Marie.

"Lyra!" exclaimed Sayre angrily.

"I've heard you cough," said Marie with concern. "It doesn't sound normal."

"I'm not going to the hospital again," said Sayre crossly.

"We do have a doctor in town," said Marie.

Sayre looked at Marie and Lyra's concerned faces.

"I'll consider it," she said. "For now, drop it."

They visited the General Store again the following week. Marie was enjoying the company of the other young women and their developing friendship.

"Next time you come you can sleep over," said Marie. "There's a spare room upstairs."

"Oh my goodness, it's okay," said Sayre. "We wouldn't do that to you."

"It's fine! I'd love to have you over for the night. And cook you breakfast in the morning," said Marie.

Sayre squeezed her hand happily. She could feel Marie's warmth and friendliness, without a trace of pity. "Thank you," she said.

The days passed pleasantly at the cabin. Spring

flowers grew along the roads and there were posies to brighten up the room. Lyra and Sayre shook the dust out of everything and mended the old blankets. There were warm soups in the evenings and when they visited Marie she played records on an old hand-crank player. Sayre felt as though for the first time in her life she could relax. She had expected to be lonely out there in the cabin, or terrified to be trapped with only her own thoughts for company, but it was serene.

Too bad we can't spend the winter, she thought.

They packed up things for overnight and went to Marie's for a sleepover.

Marie roasted up a chicken for dinner, with greens from her greenhouse, knobby potatoes from the cold house, and the end of last year's corn. The table was set with candles in tin pots punched with designs that danced along the walls and ceiling along to Carol King's Tapestry album on an ancient record player.

"You didn't have to do all this," said Sayre as she entered the magical room.

"Don't worry, this is for me too," laughed Marie. "Sit."

They ate a delicious meal and chatted.

Marie asked Lyra about her plans for the future.

"Well I'd like to travel and see more of the world..." said Lyra. "When we went to Goreham last winter, it was kind of disappointing though."

Marie laughed. "I can imagine," she said.

"I'd like to try New York City one day."

"I went to art school in New York City," said Marie.

"And you came back here?" blinked Lyra. She spent so much time thinking about how to leave that she couldn't imagine trying to come back.

"Yes. I loved school, and I learned a lot about art, but I realized I like peace and quiet for my arts practice."

"Is that where you became a tinsmith?" asked Lyra.

Marie laughed. She stood up and led them into the living room where there were paintings all over the walls.

"I did some of these in art school," she said. "But my grandmother taught me tinsmithing when I was your age. When I came back here, I rediscovered the joy of it."

Sayre and Lyra came as often as they could to Marie's house. It was a warm and welcoming place. Sayre felt incredibly safe, maybe the safest she had ever felt in her life. Marie was a strong and self-sufficient woman. Sayre wished that they had met long ago. She knew that if they ran into trouble in the winter, Marie would help them out.

Sayre gave back as best she could. She helped Marie make a huge batch of goats-milk soap, and she and Lyra helped with slaughtering and preparing animals for eating and trading in the General Store.

One morning Sayre woke up choking again. Marie insisted that they visit the doctor. The news was not good.

"You have cancer," he said. "I don't have the diagnostic tools to say for sure, but I just know. You have cancer, likely in your throat, lungs, and maybe more. It's quite advanced."

Sayre felt numb. *Just my luck,* she thought. Life always caught up with her the moment she stopped running.

"I need a damn cigarette," she said.

"No mommy, no…" said Lyra.

"Aww, baby, it'll be okay," she said, holding Lyra in her arms and rubbing her back.

"Thank you doctor, we'll take the best care of her we can with the time she has left," said Marie quietly. Sayre's breathing became more and more difficult, until she could hardly draw in enough air. Lyra spent every day by her mother's side, wiping her brow, feeding her, bringing her tingling teas to soothe her ragged throat, and helping with Sudbina. At the back of her mind she thought her mother would get better, and she could hardly imagine her being gone forever from the world, like Papa Gilles.

Sayre spent her last days in bed at Marie's house. Finally the day came when death hung in the air like a waiting spirit.

Sayre's breaths were gurgling and shallow. The end was near.

Lyra wanted to be strong in this moment, but she couldn't hold back her tears.

"We only get so much time on Earth, Lyra."

Lyra cried out, flinging her arms around her mother's neck and sobbing for the first time since she was a baby. She cried for Papa Gilles, for Sayre, and for baby Sudbina who wouldn't know her mother.

"It's okay, it's okay, shhh…" crooned Sayre, "I won't get to see Sudbina grow up..." Her voice cracked for a moment but she got it under control. "But I know you'll take wonderful care of her. You're so smart, Lyra. You're smarter than me at your age. I wasn't much older than you are now when I had Brandon. I think you'll do a much better job than I did."

"No mumma, no…" cried Lyra. She kissed her mother's cheeks over and over until Sayre's spirit was gone from her body.

CHAPTER 11: Lyra

The people in Randolph allowed Sayre to be buried in their little graveyard at the edge of town. The logistics of bringing her body anywhere else for burial were impossible, so Lyra was grateful. A few locals helped dig the hole. Burial required community.

This time was different than Papa Gilles. He burned all up and it was easy to imagine his spirit flying up to heaven or some other dimension where he was a light being or joining Gaia deep in the heart-fires of Earth. Watching the dirt fall over Sayre, so small and cold all wrapped up in a shroud made Lyra feel like she couldn't breathe.

"Wait!" she cried out. She had a sudden terrible feeling that her mother was still alive, that they were burying her alive. She reached down and touched her mother's shoulder one last time. It was cold and hard.

She stepped back and nodded tearfully. They continued shoveling dirt over her, the dark clumps cascading down until her legs were covered, her head,

her whole body. Lyra cried rivers, awkward unfamiliar
sounds coming out of her. Sudbina sucked her fingers in
Marie's arms, frowning.

Lyra and Starlight struck out on the highway from
Randolph. She needed to see the White Mountain Free
Zone, desperately hoping for a place where she and
Sudbina could be part of a loving community. She left
Sudbina with Marie while she was gone.

"You don't need to do this," said Marie. "You can
stay here."

"I can't," said Lyra. "I have to see if it's there."

Marie searched the girl's face. She knew it would be
a dangerous journey and White Mountain Free Zone was
probably not what Lyra imagined it was. She sighed.

"I hope you find what you're looking for."

"Thank you." Lyra could hear the doubts, but also
care in Marie's voice.

"I'll take good care of Sudbina."

Lyra felt intense *hiraeth*, nostalgic longing for
something imagined so real that it was like she could
taste it, or hold it in her hands, but she had never seen it
in real life. She thought about living in Androscoggin
Free Zone, but she knew she was too young and Basquiat
and the others didn't want a little girl and a baby tagging
along on their adult fun. Besides; she felt deep in her
heart that she was meant to be somewhere else.

White Mountain National Forest had featured in
Lyra's dreams since her earliest recollections. She was
compelled to go there by something deep inside her, and
now was the time. She knew by now that no community
was perfect, but she hoped this Free Zone just South
of the sacred place she had visited as a child would be
perfect for her and her sister, and a place worth living in.

CHAPTER 12: Brandon

Brandon had a motorcycle now. He had earned it; on a trip down south with the Boyz, they commandeered it from a lone rider on the road. The man he rode shotgun with traded up, and Brandon got the old bike. While riding shotgun, he was forced to submit to abuse any time the man wanted as part of his initiation into the gang.

"You don't think those Care Movement bros aren't doing the same thing? Power comes at a cost, little man."

He tried to imagine Pastor Ned hurting someone and he could not. He wasn't going to argue though. And besides, he could hardly stand up and his thoughts were swirling around his head like a toilet flush.

He drowned out the memories with revs of his motorcycle engine. He went faster and faster down the highway, so fast that his eyes hurt. It felt good.

Like Lyra, Brandon always felt that there was something beyond Dummer Mobile Home Park waiting for him in the great wide world. There was a whole land to be explored in the Kingdom of Coos County and now he would see all of it.

He and the Boyz were headed to Brandon's first major raid. They had received intel through the Rebels network that there would be a major government hit on the Free Zones. Free Zones were these communities who thought they were above the law. Some were hippy communes, some were very practical permaculture organizations, and once in while one was a neo-conservative hellhole. Any community whose leadership was operating outside government jurisdiction or arrangement would be heavily punished. The war with Russia was getting more intense. Many countries occupied by American troops had decided that it was time for the occupation to end and sided with Russia. This global anxiety made the Supreme Leader very insecure and he was determined to conquer domestic insurrection. He would make an example of the Free Zones, and it was New Hampshire's turn to be purged.

The Free Zones were mostly in better shape than state-run communities and the Boyz told Brandon there would be food stores, vehicles, and even weapons for the taking in the disarray after a government purge. The Dummer Boyz called it 'Payday'. Brandon was ready.

Some of the other gangs in the Kingdom of Coos would be joining them. They were all gang Boyz under the loose leadership of Rebel Banger Jones. The Dummer Boyz were one of many smaller gangs. Rumour had it that this Free Zone was wildly rich and there would be spoils for all.

"And women," cackled the man who had abused Brandon, a hairy guy in his fifties named Paul the Enforcer. Rape was not openly advocated amongst the Boyz, and some of them would never do it, but they would not stop another brother from doing it. Paul the Enforcer was a shameless perpetrator in this don't ask, don't tell culture.

Motorcycles revved in the distance.

"The Dixville Boyz!" roared Massacre Mike.

They rode to meet their brothers where the highways connected.

That night they camped out at a roadside motel alongside two other gangs. They were waiting for the last group, the Lancaster Boyz, to join them. They were drunk as skunks, standing around a barrel fire.

"Dummer Boyz so desperate they're taking on kids now?" said a large leather-clad man with a red beard.

Trust me, he's a man!" shouted Paul. Some men turned away and drank more, while others leered at Brandon with interest. He knew he would have to fight someone to avoid being targeted at this gathering. He peered around the circle, spying another young guy who looked like the Rosie had just whupped him hard. He was skinny with sallow skin. Brandon would pick a fight with him later. He was starting to figure out how all this fraternity stuff worked.

"Hey Pansy Ass," said Smack. Brandon winced. Pansy Ass was a nickname he was desperate to ditch. "You're going to scout for us. As soon as the feds show up, you race back here and tell us."

Brandon considered. *That won't be so bad,* he thought.

He gave a curt nod. No one said no to Smack anyway.

Brandon went ahead on his bike to White Mountain Free Zone. The road was eerily familiar because he had been down it once before as a little boy. To get to the Free Zone he would have to go further than he had ever been.

Furthest away from home in my whole family, he thought smugly. He knew they hated that he had chosen gang life, but eventually they would see the benefits. After the raid he would cruise back into Dummer Mobile Home Park and show that fat Mustang Dougie and everyone else what kind of a man he was, with all the

spoils he would bring home. He felt a pang of nostalgia
thinking of home. Admittedly, he missed his mother, and
that old Papa Gilles. He even missed Lyra a little bit.
Then he remembered that she would probably still hate
him for stealing her dog.

"Come on, Monster," he called, slowing down to
a stop on the bike. He had renamed the dog Monster.
The dog trotted up. He was still a puppy, but huge like
his mother. He could run like the dickens. He panted,
catching his breath.

"Good boy," crooned Brandon in a rare moment of
tenderness. He couldn't talk like that around the Boyz or
they'd punish him.

Suddenly the dog was tense. Brandon looked
around.

Off in the distance, two tiny figures were running.
The chase instinct kicked in and man and dog shot
forward.

Brandon cruised down the highway. A young woman
and her dog were running away from him. She turned at
the sound of the motorcycle rev and jumped off the road.
Brandon felt a shiver of shock. It was his sister, Lyra.

What the hell is she up to? thought Brandon.

He revved hard, enjoying scaring the crap out of her.

"Get her!" he shouted to Monster, who took off into
the field.
He pulled over his motorcycle.

"Lyra!" he called. "Lyra!" he didn't want to chase
after her in the field.

Starlight was running with Lyra, and then she turned
back and ran the other way.

"Starlight!" said Lyra crossly, but nothing could stop
her from running to greet her pup.

Lyra couldn't help but smile when she saw Grease
Lightnin and Starlight pouncing and rolling on each other
with pure joy. She looked up and saw the tall skinny
figure of Brandon at the roadside.

So much has happened since I saw you last, she thought.

"Come here!" he shouted.

"What do you want?" she yelled. She looked up and down the road. There was nowhere to go. Her bicycle was in the ditch just a few steps from Brandon, where she had dumped it as soon as she heard the motorcycle rev.

"Come on!" he shouted. He leaned on his bike and waited.

Lyra looked at the dogs prancing happily in the field.

She looked at her brother long and hard. She thought about Sayre and Papa Gilles. He didn't know, and she felt pity for him. She decided to give Brandon one last chance, for her family's sake. She walked up from the field, the dogs dancing along behind her.

"Hello Brandon," she said. She looked him up and down. He was taller. His remaining baby fat was gone, and his face had a man's shape.

"Hi mousie," he said. He really meant to use Papa Gilles' name for her affectionately but it came out derisively.

Lyra's face was impassive.

"What are you doing?" she asked.

"What does it look like?" he patted his motorcycle proudly.

"What did you do to get that?" she asked coldly. She meant that he must have stolen it, but his defences flared.

"You wouldn't understand," he snarled.

Lyra grabbed her bicycle and got on it.

"Come on, Starlight," she called.

"Where are you going?"

"Home."

"Home is the other way." Brandon frowned.

Then realization dawned on him. His sister had been talking about White Mountain National Forest all her life, and since she got twigged on Joan Whiteduck, she had been talking about the Free Zones. She was going there.

"You can't go there," he said.

"Where?"

"White Mountain Free Zone."

"Why not?"

"The government is planning to blow it up. Any day now."

"You're lying!"

"No I'm not."

"How would you know?"

"I'm out scouting for the Boyz," he said. "After the feds light it up, we're going in for a raid."

He turned to look at Lyra. She looked furious.

Probably shouldn't have said that last part, he thought.

"I don't believe you," she said, but he could tell by her voice that she did.

She pedalled faster.

"Hey! Stop!"

"No!"

Brandon jogged back to his motorcycle and hopped on. He followed her.

It wasn't far, so he decided to stick with Lyra.

Annoy her a little longer, he thought. The truth was, he missed her. He missed home, and the safe company of women.

They came to a cheerful rainbow-painted sign on the highway. *White Mountain Free Zone This Way.*

Lyra smiled and turned down the trail.

"I'm telling you, it's all over," said Brandon. "They're getting the axe."

"Shut up."

"It's the New World Order," said Brandon.

"It's not the New World Order," snapped Lyra. "The world isn't like this! It's just us!"

Brandon just squinted at her. He had never read a book, and to him Coos County was the world, and Coos County order might as well be the world order.

They came to a cheerful town square.

"Hello travellers," said a man in a long patchwork

coat. Reasonably clean, well-fed children chased each other nearby. "What brings you here?"

A few others stopped to see who was here. They eyed the chopper with warranted suspicion. Lyra's presence calmed their worries. The gangs were homosocial groups that didn't allow women.

"Hello," said Lyra. "I'm afraid I have bad news."

"Lyra!" hissed Brandon between his teeth. *She's going to tell them,* he thought. *She's going to just go ahead and fucking tell them.* He felt a flash of anger.

A little boy bumped into him, chased by another. Brandon looked down and his eyes met the boy's. The little one smiled and ran off, followed by his friend.

If she doesn't tell them, all these people will die, he realized. All the raids he had done so far were on places like Mustang Dougie's trailer. No one was seriously hurt unless they fought back, and they knew the drill by now.

These people are totally innocent, he thought. *They have no idea what they're in for.* He looked around and saw women, children, and elders enjoying the town square freely.

Lyra told them everything she knew. They called more townsfolk to join the conversation.

"We have to make preparations to leave," exclaimed one.

"Are we seriously going to listen to a pair of ragtaggle teenagers?" said another.

"We've heard rumours like this before."

"Do what you have to do," said Lyra sadly. "But it's not safe here."

"I believe them," said an old woman, coming forward. She was wise, and everyone listened. "This has happened before, you know," she said. "We have survived this before, and we will again." There was a large indigenous community at White Mountain Free Zone who had experienced being targeted, in some way or another, by settlers, every generation. "We should make a plan. Where should we hide?"

The Free Zone council decided to make preparations to send the children and willing adults out of the village and far into the forest. There was a bluff, high on a ridge, where they could watch, unseen, for intruders.

"You're not going with them…" said Brandon as Lyra made to follow.

"Yes I am."

"Lyra, don't be stupid. Go home."

"Come with us, Brandon."

"You know I can't. Once the soldiers come you know what I have to do."

"You don't have to do anything. Do what's right, Brandon!"

"Go home!"

"There is no home!" she cried. "Mummy and Papa Gilles are dead. There's nothing left in Dummer."

Brandon felt his breath constrict. He was stunned.

"This is your last chance Brandon. This is your last chance for family. If you go now, you'll never see me again."

"You don't understand. If I don't go back to the Boyz, there will be nowhere safe for me. Anywhere. I have no choice."

"Come with me away from all this. I'm going to find Joan. And help her."

"Joan?" Brandon scowled.

"Yes. I want to live in a place where people don't have to choose between food or healthcare, or burn to death in their sleep, or get bombed, " she said. "I want to live somewhere where people help each other, and are safe." Her heart ached for the people of the White Mountain Free Zone, packing their bags to hide while their town was under attack.

"That place doesn't exist."

"It does! And if it doesn't I want to build it."

"That's not how the world works!"

"Yes it is!"

Lyra trudged off after the others up through the forest

to the bluff.

Why does she have to ruin everything? thought Brandon angrily.

He rode off on his motorcycle.

I have to go back to the Dummer Boyz. It's what I've always wanted.

Thoughts of doubt swirled in his head. He knew they were his best option.

Are Mum and Gilles really dead? he wondered. He could hardly believe that was possible.

CHAPTER 13: Lyra

Just hours after they reached the bluff, Lyra and the people of White Mountain Free Zone watched their country's military unleash fire and brimstone on the village in the valley below. Their helpless wails of disbelief reminded Lyra of the aftermath of the fire in Dummer Mobile Home Park. After the military retreated, the drone of motorcycles permeated the air. The gangs descended on the burning town. The men feasted and ransacked for days while the folks on the mountain watched in fear.

CHAPTER 14: Brandon

Brandon returned to the Dummer Boyz after all. He didn't want to raid the village like that, but it was his job to come back from scouting and give the signal.

There was nothing to be done, he thought.

Lyra had completely ruined the raid for him. Now he halfheartedly opened doors and cupboards in the rubble, feeling guilty thinking about the people whose lives they were tearing apart.

Some of the men were taking pleasure in tormenting the community survivors. Brandon had no stomach for that whatsoever and stayed as far away as possible.

Brandon still did not believe that his mother could really be dead. In the back of his mind, he kept worrying about her. He wanted to go to Dummer and see for himself.

He stood up from the pile of clothes he was rifling through, pulling off his pants to try on a pair of clean jeans. They fit decent enough. He put his shoes back on.

I hope we can get out of this place soon, thought

Brandon. He never wanted to come here again.

He walked back the way he came. This town was very easy to navigate; the paths were circular, leading to the centre. In the town square there was a carnage of male violence too brutal to describe comfortably. They were the Goths sacking little Romes, after the Republic had collapsed into itself. Brandon let his eyes go slack, trying to avoid taking anything in and passing through quickly.

He stumbled over something and he looked down as he was righting himself. It was the crumpled body of the sweet-smiling little boy who ran into him in this square this morning. Brandon grimaced and fell backward.

There was something cold and hard under him. He looked down to see, there in the dirt of the town square, there was a large flat stone which read:

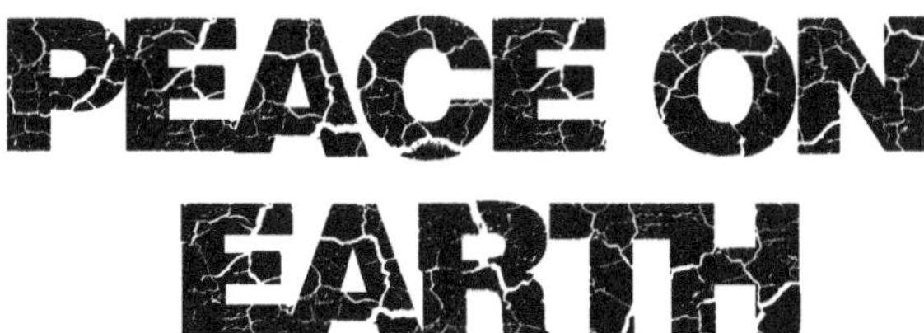

Tears stung the corners of his eyes. The mask of cognitive dissonance began to crack. He blinked and looked around the square, fully opening himself to the empathy repressed deep inside him. He saw whimpering women, pulling their clothes around them. He saw food silos pierced, their care-harvested grains spilling needlessly away. Flame-charred smouldering ruins of things burned: houses, gardens, people. The little boy, so generous with his magic smile, now lifeless on the ground.

I hate these men, he thought.

The thought grew louder. "I hate these men," he murmured. He was in shock.

Why would I want to be like them? Must I spend my whole life doing this? And Brandon imagined his life. It flashed before his very eyes. He saw himself perpetrating acts of violence on people his whole life in one endless chain of destruction until someone ended up killing him.

Brandon was crying uncontrollably. The men in the square began to notice. Brandon was completely checked out of his body, and traveling in some other dimension.

I will leave these men, he thought.

Then, he was plagued by doubt. *But where will I go? If Lyra is right, and there are good places, then I could go there… but Lyra must be wrong. There can't be good places. It's like this everywhere. This is the best there is. I'll be stuck trying to get in with a new gang, with a traitor reputation.* Again he imagined in a flash, a memory-like transmission of prophecy showing an alternate future.

I can't live like this. A feeling like wanting to give up crept up inside him.

What do I have to live for? He could think of nothing.

He had nothing to live for.

Did he know anyone with something to live for?

Lyra. Brandon scoffed in his mind's eye imagining Lyra's quiet persistence. She believed in Joan, and in a better world.

Sayre… Then he thought suddenly of his mother. *Did she have anything to live for? No,* he thought, *she didn't.* He resented her. He resented that he was always alone as a kid, until Lyra came around, he resented that other boys made fun of him about his mother's way to make ends meet for them, made fun of Lyra, his solemn-eyed sister. *Sayre… What did you have to live for?* The answer donged into his brain like a giant bell.

She had you. She had you to live for. And he finally let his heart break for his mother.

"Sayre…" he cried out in the square, completely unaware of the men gathering around him as he sobbed jibberish.

He was worth living for.

I am worth living for.

Tears of gratitude rolled down his cheeks. He laughed out loud.

Mum lived for Lyra and me, he thought. *She lived for us.*

His heart cracked open, glowing with a golden light, so much love suddenly flowing through it.

"Monster," he laughed. "I love that damn dog more than anything…"

And he thought of all the things he loved and smiled. In that moment he was pure love.

The men kicked Brandon until his head was bloody pulp.

A beautiful memory flashed before Brandon's eyes, a different future in an alternate reality. He followed Lyra up the mountain and followed her North to be with Joan, and fell in love with Joan, and they were a lovely family. Brandon's spirit followed the beautiful memory out into space, and left his body behind just as he was having a spiritual awakening.

The men carried on their way and left Pansy Ass dead in the town square at Free Zone Raid 2. Some wondered where his dog went.

"Where's Pansy Ass?" asked Paul the Enforcer.

"Too young, he couldn't hack it," they said.

CHAPTER 15: Lyra

Lyra watched in stony horror from the bluff as her brother was beaten to death.

Was she destined to watch her entire family die before her eyes?

She couldn't cry. Today was too much, and she was numb with overwhelm. She would have to mourn her only brother later.

White Mountain Free Zone was not Lyra's destiny and she knew it now.

"Please bury my brother with your dead," she asked the survivors as they trekked back down the bluff.

Then she got back on her bicycle and left, with Starlight and Grease Lightnin following along behind her. She was headed back to Randolph. Sudbina was all the family she had left in this world.

Lyra and the dogs got as far as they could before sundown, and then they bedded down in a deep ditch outside a town for the night.

In the morning, Lyra took a detour into the town. She was still in shock from what she had seen, and although she mostly hated people she also really wanted the company of good ones and she was determined to find some, even at her peril. She nipped into an Inn. There was a saloon in the front where several folks were eating baked beans and eggs for breakfast. Lyra sidled up to a large wooden bar where screens were playing the news. She watched with interest as reports covered happenings in the city centres.

Suddenly the familiar profile of White Mountain Free Zone appeared on the screen.

Militants neutralized at White Mountain Free Zone, reported the news.

Lyra grimaced and turned away. She couldn't watch.

The grimy old man beside her at the bar caught her eye.

"Heyo there girlie," he said. He smelled of sour booze. "It's my birthday."

"Happy Birthday," said Lyra quietly.

"Is Old Willy bugging you?" said the barmaid, coming over.

"No, it's fine."

"Alright well if he does, just let me know."

"Thanks."

"If you could have anything for your birthday, what would it be?" asked Old Willy with a woozy smile.

"I'd take a hot meal for starters," laughed Lyra.

The old man gabbled on about cigarettes and Lyra's mind drifted away in thought.

What would I ask for if I could have anything in the world I wanted? she thought. She felt so small and powerless to be able to do anything... for herself or anyone else.

Suddenly Old Willy's voice was sharp. Lyra's focus snapped back to the moment at hand.

"That little slut," he hissed, looking up at the screen above the bar.

Lyra looked up to see Joan's sombre round face looking at the camera defiantly. Her arms and legs were chained up to a giant billboard that read:

END OIL SUPREMACY

She was hanging there naked as thousands of people screamed below, some bloodthirsty and others supportive as cameras flashed. Someone threw a bottle and it smashed on the sign, narrowly missing Joan's head. She squeezed her eyes shut and flinched as chips of glass sprayed her face. Her expression never changed.

Lyra's breath caught in her throat.

If I could do anything in the world, she thought, *it would be to be there with Joan to help her.*

On the television screen, Joan started to speak and the crowd below stilled to listen. Lyra leaned in expectantly, but Old Willy kept mumbling obscenities and she couldn't hear.

"Shush," she said curtly. He shut up.

"End oil supremacy. End the oil wars. End the destruction of Mother Earth. End capitalism. End plastic. End corporate ownership of land," cried Joan from high up on the billboard. "This system is all wrong. The next world is ours for the making."

Lyra knew deep in her heart that Joan was right. A better world was not going to happen unless good people made it happen. As she looked up at Joan, naked and vulnerable but so powerful in her conviction, Lyra knew the time had come. She would find Joan and pledge her life to Joan's cause. She stood up.

"Happy Birthday," she said to Old Willy on her way out.

Lyra made her way back to the bike in the ditch with

the dogs and they continued on their way. They would reach Randolph soon. Lyra was anxious to hold Sudbina in her arms.

As she entered town, Lyra had a bad feeling. Something was wrong.

"Marie," said Lyra. "What's going on?"

Everyone in town was sick with unnatural boils. The odd part was that it struck everybody in the village but a few people in the surrounding hills who had come into contact with the villagers were unaffected.

After a few days of trying to get to the bottom of it, they figured it out.

"The Company poisoned the river."

The dam development Joan was talking about finally destroyed their water source.

The local Council held a sombre meeting. The town could hardly survive with no drinkable water. The science and equipment to treat the water existed, but no one here could afford or access it. The unthinkable had happened and now they would all have to move.

"I don't know what to do," said Marie. She was heartbroken.

"Let's go North and find Joan," said Lyra passionately.

Marie's brow creased. She had built so much here, with her tinsmith shop and reviving her grandmother's old General Store in Randolph. To leave would be terrible.

"Can't we go to one of those free zones you were talking about?"

"The free zones are dangerous," said Lyra. "We need to go far, far away."

"How do you know there is a safe place?"

"I don't know," said Lyra. "I believe."

Sudbina cried.

"And how will Sudbina make a journey North?" said Marie as she went off to soothe the baby.

"I don't know," cried Lyra. Suddenly she sounded like a little girl.

Marie came back into the room.

"Aww, I'm sorry Lyra, I didn't mean to upset you."

"I don't know anything," said Lyra.

Marie hugged her.

"Everything's going to be okay," she said.

"Really?"

"Yes. Let's go follow Joan."

Marie packed up her treasures- the tools of her trade- her tinsnips and favourite iron.

"For a fresh start," she said.

They packed up provisions onto Marie's two horses.

"They can't survive without clean water either so they're not staying here," said Marie. Lyra had done a little riding on visits with Marie. This would be a challenge.

Starlight and Grease Lightnin trotted alongside.

CHAPTER 16: Joan

Joan's journey of actions across the continent had taken her south of the Canadian-American border, and now she was winding her way back up into the northern part of her territory.

The crossing agents were giving her a hard time.

"You can't just leave. You get to leave when we say you get to leave."

"I am not leaving anything," she said calmly. "I'm walking through my own traditional territory."

An agent came over and pulled aside the one arguing with Joan. They went into a room to have a heated discussion. It appeared that someone realized who she was. The question was, did today's agents want to teach her some kind of lesson, or would they just want to be rid of her?

"We can't just let her do whatever she wants," said one crossly.

"Do you see that camera filming us? Just get her the fuck out of here as fast as possible. Let Canada deal with her."

Joan was sent expeditiously on her way.

St. Andrews, New Brunswick was not far from the 'border' crossing and Joan arrived at the rally planned by the local EcoClub right on time.

"People of Qonasqamkuk!" she called out from the microphone to the gathered crowd. "The Ancient Fireplace!"

The crowd cheered.

"I have come to the traditional territory of my mother, Aniapsuin."

A bus from a nunnery drove up and unloaded. Nuns joined the crowd holding their posters of support.

At one time Joan thought she might join a religious order. Cloistered life in a community of women sounded appealing to her. She showed up to a meeting for a preliminary interview and it was not what she thought it would be. There were radical nuns but still they did not go far enough for her. They didn't understand that the earth couldn't wait. Still, this other kind of vow to protect Mother Earth was a kind of holy devotion as radical as the path of ascetic life.

"We gather here on the traditional territory of the Mikmaq, who tended this beautiful garden for thousands of years, preserving nature's balance with all living things, and clean air, and food and medicine for all," began Joan in her powerful and commanding voice. The audience listened in rapt attention. "When Samuel de Champlain visited over 20 communities along the St. Croix River in 1604, he wrote that these villages had about 1000 residents each, and these people were tall, energetic, healthy, muscular people organized with a distinct culture and government. Our elders lived to be over 100 years old. Champlain had never seen anything like it before- in the place he came from, he would be lucky to reach 36 years old. 1 out of 10 of his European sailors had birth defects from chronic malnourishment, disease, war, and incest. Their society was stratified between the rich and the peasants. Our people shared food, education, healthcare… there was not a single medicine plant on this land that we didn't understand, cultivate, honour, and use. Thousands of years of peace and agricultural innovation organized our communities for living the best possible life. Champlain saw this, and was amazed."

Joan looked out over the crowd. By now many Canadians understood the lies and fake history of colonialism, but with every generation this knowledge sunk in deeper.

"Later, the British called us savages," continued Joan. "But we were not the savages. We shared generously of our food, our homes, our medicines, and our deep wisdom. We lifted up the poor, the malnourished, the uncivilized Europeans. But the settlers brought their rulers too. The incest-mad royals and their armies, who commanded through fear and destruction. The colonizers imposed their broken system on us. They scarred this land. They tore our people apart. We are still healing. Much healing is left to be done. The ancestors are warning us, and our descendants inspire us. We must be courageous. We must stand up for what every child knows is good. We must care for one another."

Joan reached into her bag and pulled something out.

"I told you to come here bringing a heart-shaped piece of trash." Joan held up a bottle-green lump of plastic formed into a heart shape. She nodded to folks standing to the side of the popup stage. "I have helpers who will support with construction of our monument."

Joan had connected with a local community arts club who were supporting the installation of a Community Arts monument. They had heat guns for fusing plastics, drills, saws, construction glue, and unlike some of Joan's more controversial actions, they had secured all the appropriate permissions from the city. The artists built a wooden structure and the gathered crowd was working in clusters to create heart pieces to affix to the broken heart monument.

"Go now and start building. I'm going to come down and meet all of you."

The field became a bustle of activity as everyone worked on their small part. Joan descended the stage and walked from group to group, chatting with those who gathered to participate in the Community Arts installation.

One petite woman stood alone off to the side holding a heart carved out of a water bottle.

"Come join a group," called Joan.

The woman smiled shyly and walked hesitantly over.

"Let's get this into the installation," said Joan.

They walked together to the wooden frame where the artists were melting and burning things together.

The woman stepped in and her nimble fingers helped where needed.

The groups came over one by one and the monument took shape.

"What do you think?" asked Joan to the woman standing quietly beside her.

The woman looked up at the giant form for a long moment.

"It's crazy how long we built out of wood, and how much damage plastic has done to the environment and our health in such a short little time..."

Joan grinned. "Wood is incredible, isn't it? Why do we love plastic so much?"

The artists, up on tall ladders, made the final attachments.

"Everyone!" said Joan into her loudspeaker. "Let's clean up the field!"

The crowd milled around, picking up debris or bits that were left.

"Hey, want to go for dinner with us?" Joan asked the quiet woman.

"Sure."

The organizers all went out for a special meal together at a local restaurant.

"Thank you so much for helping to bring my vision to life," said Joan.

"Our pleasure," laughed one of the artists.

They chatted amiably and enjoyed good food. The artists explained how progressive St. Andrews was on climate protection, and all of the green initiatives the community had achieved with good municipal leadership. One particularly progressive City Council in the 2030s had been elected and implemented a visionary strategic plan for the community's future. They re-structured the city for long-term sustainability and now the fruits of that labour were evident in the beautiful clean little city.

"I'd love a tour," said Joan. "Would you take me?" she asked, turning to the quiet woman beside her.

"I'm new here too."

"We'd definitely take you," said one of the artists.

"Let's do that tomorrow!" They all agreed to take Joan out the next day to check out St. Andrews.

They all parted ways and went off for the night.

Joan returned to her hotel, and was surprised to see the quiet woman from earlier today in the lobby.

"Well hello," she exclaimed.

"Hi," said the woman with warm surprise.

"Right, you said you were also from out of town."

"Yes, just visiting."

"How did you know about the event?"

The woman pointed to a poster nearby in the lobby. "I saw that and got intrigued."

Joan laughed.

"Want to sit in the lounge with me for a bit? I'm not quite ready for bed."

"I'd love to."

They went over to the lounge. The woman was obviously shy, but she was warm and the silence was not awkward.

"I'm Joan by the way, nice to meet you."

"I'm Apollo."

Apollo was visiting the beautiful port town of St. Andrews on vacation. To Joan's surprise, she was an award-winning scientist and Nova Scotia native. Joan was amazed how young she was to be so centred in purpose. She rarely met people formidable like herself.

As they talked and got to know each other, Apollo's personality blossomed. She was hard to read at first, but now that she felt more comfortable with Joan, she was telling deadpan jokes with sparkling eyes and Joan was belly-laughing. Apollo beamed. Joan was bringing out a side of her that most people didn't see.

They talked well into the night.

Finally it was ridiculously late and they were tired. They decided to go to bed and meet for breakfast in the morning.
Apollo went to sleep with glowing content; she felt that in Joan she had met a friend for life.

When Joan woke up in the morning something had changed. She felt a current of excitement. When the alarm sounded she hopped out of bed and went to the shower with a pep in her step. She spent a few extra minutes getting ready. She felt like she really wanted to look nice today.

Joan went down to the breakfast room at the hotel. There was Apollo, sitting by the window sipping her espresso. She was so cute and cool. Apollo turned over to look and her eyes met Joan's. Joan felt her heart flutter. She walked over.

"Good morning."

"Good morning."

Joan looked over Apollo's face with morning eyes. She was pretty in a fresh, tomboyish way. She had short hair and very faint freckles, up close. Joan felt herself smiling.

"I got myself coffee but I'm ready to eat now if you are," said Apollo.

"Sure."

They walked over to the breakfast buffet.

As they served their meals they tried to make conversation but it was awkward for a moment between grinding smoothies and serving eggs. Once they sat down at the table, they quickly fell back into the comfortable rhythm they had established the night before.

They finished breakfast and went to the meet-up spot suggested by the arts collective, their organizing space downtown called Studio Dreamshare. They spent the day on bicycles touring around the people-friendly city. It was the kind of small solarpunk metropolis that Joan hoped more cities would aspire to evolve into in time. The city was a perfect meeting and mixing of art and science expressed in public spaces where people socialized in person. Some people wore masks as another variant of the Rosie swept the populace, but by this time the virus was only a serious danger to the most vulnerable, as the entire community had access to free vaccine boosters so their bodies were strong against the new strains.

In the afternoon, the arts collective took Joan for a sleigh ride. The city had a fleet of horse-drawn conveyance as part of their green infrastructure, particularly needed in winter when the bicycles were less efficient. Apollo was in her element amongst horses. They climbed into a carriage and sat close. Joan and Apollo were pressed tight beside two others. Joan was on the outside and Apollo had to lean over her to see outside.

"These are Ojibwe ponies," one of the artist guides told them. "Ancient North American pony genetics."

The horses were medium-small in stature with strong legs and clever eyes. The ponies spent the summer playing and relaxing in the summer sun. They grazed in the forests and fields surrounding the city, and voluntarily came into the barns in winter when food was more scarce. They had been doing this for thousands of years.

Apollo was fascinated with the horse stories and listened close. Joan watched Apollo with interest. She was crushing hard. Joan was pretty ace, and mostly not interested in dating. She was too busy and focused on other things. This girl Apollo though was just so cute and smart.

But she's a scientist and she lives far away, thought Joan. She eyed Apollo, trying to guess her age. *Probably not interested in being more than friends with someone my age...* She sighed. *Enjoy the moment.*

"Want some gum?"

"Sure," said Apollo.

Joan shared a piece with her. Their hands touched. Their eyes met.

Did she just blush a little bit? thought Joan. *Or did I imagine that?*

CHAPTER 17: Apollo and Joan

Apollo felt a wave of attraction looking into the eyes of the woman sitting next to her in the carriage. It was unexpected and raw. She had an urge to brush Joan's cheek with soft lips in appreciation. She felt by the look in Joan's eyes that it wouldn't be unwanted.

How can you be vibing with someone new? thought Apollo. She struggled for a moment with feelings of shame and disappointment that she must be dissatisfied and ungrateful for her life.

No, you just have a lot of love to give, she thought.

Her life was complicated enough without adding this. Apollo had a long-term boyfriend who she lived with, Ben, and a new roommate, Kip, who had added a confusing element to the dynamic.

Apollo felt Joan's warm hand curl around hers.

Joan Whiteduck is holding my hand, she thought, a thrill running straight through her. She gave Joan's hand a little squeeze involuntarily. Joan leaned her head on Apollo's shoulder.

They rode along in the carriage for the rest of the tour like that, high on the joy of finding a kindred spirit and a bit of affection in a mad world.

When the tour ended and they disembarked from the carriage, it all felt like a dream. They said their goodbyes to the arts collective and headed back to the hotel.

"Would you like to hang out in my hotel room?" asked Joan. She didn't want the feeling to end.

"Umm, well I'm not sure," said Apollo. She wasn't sure exactly what she wanted. She did want to hang out with Joan as much as possible, but she didn't want to get carried away.

"Okay. Up to you," smiled Joan.

Apollo felt safe. Even though they didn't know each other well, she was confident that Joan would respect her boundaries.

"Okay. I'll come over for a bit."

"We can watch a movie or something."

"Sure. Want to meet at my room in like 20 mins?"

They each went up to their rooms.

Apollo changed out of her day clothes into comfortable pyjama pants. She washed her face and then headed over to Joan's room.

They ended up watching the movie, holding hands, and having a cozy sleepover. Joan respected Apollo's space and they went to bed for the night in separate beds in Joan's suite. They chatted with the lights off, sharing stories and getting to know one another more. Joan told Apollo all about her mother, and Apollo talked a lot about the First Mother project, an innovative embryology experiment she was working on. It was a joyful novelty to have someone to talk about her research with.

Finally, Apollo asked the burning question.

"How long will you be in St. Andrews?"

"I'm going to visit my mother's relatives," said Joan. "I'm a bit nervous because I haven't seen them since I was a kid. I've changed a lot..."

"I can't imagine you being nervous about anything," said Apollo with admiration.

"How about you?"

"I'm pretty flexible," said Apollo. "I was planning to check out some other places, but this one is pretty interesting."

They both laughed. They could feel the heady attraction they had for one another. For Apollo it was an intense friendly admiration, and for Joan there was an undeniable physical element, but Joan was content spending time talking with Apollo in the bed across the room.

Finally, after hours of talking, Apollo asked if Joan wouldn't mind if she joined her.

"Of course."

Apollo climbed into the big fluffy bed beside Joan. It was easier to talk this way. They chatted and eventually fell asleep with their hands intertwined.

The next morning Joan went to visit her relatives.

Apollo booked a day at the spa. While she was there, a story played on the news; in response to Joan's illegal nude protest chained to the billboard, the Supreme Leader of the USA posted on social media that she should go back to Canada, and he wouldn't be surprised if someone murdered her if she ever came back.

Joan's follower collective responded:

You can't kill Us.

Joan posted a video from her family's yard, safe in Canada: "Scientists are documenting the extinction of planet earth. They are measuring the ongoing elimination of plants, animals, clean water, and the air we breathe. Climate Denial Fascists can't handle the discomfort of changing your ways to stop this extinction. Denial is your only mechanism of defence against the pain of caring for the fate of future generations. Cultivate courage. Cultivate life."

I just saw the news, texted Apollo. *Are you okay?*

Joan looked at the words on the bright little screen. She scanned her thoughts and feelings. Her logical brain knew that she was in danger, but as usual, she felt nothing.

I'm okay, she texted back.

Joan was used to this kind of hateful response to her protests. In fact, the Supreme Leader's statement resulted in an upsurge of Joan's followers, and a litany of derivative Actions all over the world. It was all so confusing; Joan detached herself emotionally from the responses to her work, both positive and negative. She focused on the Actions as a spiritual and artistic practice.

Joan looked back down at the bright little screen. Apollo was reaching out because she cared, not because of the work. Joan felt gratitude.

How is your relaxing spa day going? she asked.

It's fine, I'm fine...

Joan sighed and clicked off the phone screen. This flirtation with Apollo was fun, but Joan felt practically undateable.

It wouldn't be fair for me to actually date anyone, she thought. *They would have to deal with all this weird publicity all the time.* She avoided thinking about the fact that her life was subject to constant threats of male violence.

Apollo and Joan met back up later at the hotel. They had been thinking fondly of each other during the day, but suddenly in person they were shy again. Joan was deeply awkward, which Apollo mirrored, retreating to her quiet stoicism. It was a reminder that they were complete strangers, and yet their mutual admiration for one another weighed heavy in the air around them. It was confusing and pleasurable at once.

They lay on Joan's bed, Apollo curled up on Joan's shoulder. Apollo asked her about her safety, and Joan told her a bit about the kinds of threats and attacks she had endured.

Joan found this topic of conversation exhausting and mildly annoying. It felt like she was being pressed by the media.

Apollo could see Joan was uncomfortable and didn't pry. She changed the subject and talked about her love for horses, something Joan had expressed curiosity about.

Apollo was reminded of Kip, back home, whom she had taught to ride horses.

Should I tell her about Kip and Ben?

She wasn't sure if she needed to or not. It didn't seem possible that this connection with Joan could possibly lead to a relationship, with their very different lifestyles. Apollo hoped that they would stay friends, and she didn't want to ruin the moment by getting into a heavy conversation about personal relationships.

If a good moment comes up... she thought.

Joan took Apollo's hand, intertwining their fingers.

Apollo stuttered and paused her story.

"Keep going, I'm listening," said Joan. "Tell me more about your horses."

Apollo felt warm all over. She blushed and continued with her train of thought.

Joan squeezed her hand. Apollo snuggled in closer. She tilted up her chin and Joan tilted hers down, looking at Apollo. Their faces were close. Apollo felt Joan's warmth on her cheek, and breathed in the intoxicating smell she missed, the sweetness of a woman. She knew Joan's lips would be lovely, like a special fruit she hadn't tasted in a long time.

"Can I please kiss you?" asked Joan quietly.

Apollo could only nod. She was tongue tied and light headed. Some part of her thought it prudent to say no, but her mouth watered at the thought of Joan's kiss.

Before she could think too much about it, Apollo felt Joan's lips on hers. The kisses were so soft and gentle. Apollo shifted out of passive cuddle position and kissed back passionately.

Joan wrapped her arms around Apollo and squeezed her close. As they kissed she felt fireworks going off. This was like nothing she had ever felt before. She had never been kissed like this before.

Joan had never been in a relationship. She had been on a few dates, with women and men. Men who had kissed her tasted like cigarettes, stale breath, and unpleasant musk, and when she had kissed women she felt nothing but moist lips and the novelty of a new experience. She was never turned on by real people and she rarely masturbated. She thought she was probably asexual.

Kissing Apollo filled her with pleasant tingles. She revelled in the novelty as Apollo kissed her cheeks, her neck, the tips of her ears…

Apollo felt the ache of desire. She wished she had brought up Kip and Ben earlier. She wouldn't feel right taking this makeout to a more intimate place without first having that conversation.

They kissed and kissed, their energies mingling and expanding in chemical reactions. Joan's hands wandered, curious and amazed at these feelings she was having. She ran her hand along the curve of Apollo's back and squeezed her butt gently. Apollo responded by pressing her whole body hard against her. Joan felt a flash of desire.

Apollo drew back slightly. Joan felt her tense up.

"Is this okay?" she murmured between kisses.

"Yes, this is okay. Let's not go further than this," said Apollo.

Joan nodded. They kissed passionately late into the night and fell asleep in each other's arms.

The next morning Joan and Apollo continued where they left off, entwined in one another's warmth. Their lips quickly found one another as they awoke in the hotel room.

Apollo was amazed at these feelings. This dizzying

sensation she had looking into Joan's eyes was like nothing she had ever felt before. She and Ben had always been good friends and great housemates, and overall comfortable and safe together. With Kip, it was intensely passionate and fun, but not deep. He drove her into a frenzy of desire, but after making love to him she needed her distance and space. Joan was brilliant and creative, and also beautiful. Apollo loved how they could talk for hours, and Joan was smart enough to talk about things that interested Apollo, something rare for her outside of her scientist family.

Apollo knew she would have to return to her work soon. She was avoiding it, but she couldn't leave Dr. Crystal to do everything for much longer. Part of her wanted to keep things uncomplicated and sweet between herself and Joan, and part of her knew she would regret it, possibly for life, if she didn't follow her desires. Apollo felt the ache of missing a woman's touch. Her first experiences were with women, and then she had met Ben. She missed how women kissed, and their smooth skin and curves. She longed to touch Joan's naked skin.

They kissed and kissed. Apollo felt her passions rise again. In the warm pile of blankets, in the unfamiliar hotel room far from home, she felt a twinge of guilt for not mentioning Ben and Kip, and then she gave in to her passion.

"I think I'm ready to go further," she murmured.

Joan swallowed. She didn't really know what Apollo wanted.

"Tell me what you need," she said. "I'm all yours."

The two women spent the morning in bed, spending hours enjoying each other's beauty, rising in intensity to give each other orgasms, and falling into relaxed conversations and cuddles, and then doing it all over again. There was no beginning and no end, simply warm and wet love-making fuelled by mutual admiration until they were both hungry for lunch.

They finally dragged themselves out of bed to find

something to eat.

Apollo glowed with the deep relaxation of being fully satisfied in a way rare or impossible with a man or by herself. Every nerve in her body was singing from repeated stimulation from her root chakra outwards.

Joan felt like she was floating on a cloud. This was her first time orgasming with a partner. She had never felt comfortable enough with another person to get even close to this point. She tingled to her fingertips.

She cast a sidelong look at Apollo.

Is this love? she thought.

CHAPTER 18: Lyra and Marie

The last Lyra heard, Joan was in St. Andrews, New Brunswick. They would have to travel East through unfamiliar lands to cross the USA-Canada national border to get to her. It would be faster to journey on the highways, but then they ran the risk of encountering gangs and other dangerous men. Just East of Coos County there was a small self-declared kingdom called Gilead where women were forced to be breeding slaves, or so it was rumoured.

"We'll ride along the Appalachian Trail," said Marie. "It should only be a few days by horse from here to the Canadian border, and we can avoid all sorts of trouble."

The trail was well travelled and groomed, even in these strange times. There were fields of long grasses for the horses and good places to rest. Lyra was lucky to be travelling with Marie, who had all the gear for tent-camping at night. The views were beautiful and Lyra couldn't believe this was so close to her home her whole life.

And now I'm leaving it behind, she thought. She wondered if she would ever see her homeland again.

"Have you ever seen such a thing?" asked Lyra with wonder at the sight of Old Speck.

"I've seen it before," laughed Marie. "But it is beautiful. Haven't you?"

Lyra's life so far had been a lot different than Marie's. No, she had not hiked on the trail before, and she didn't even know it existed for that matter. Already this journey had taken her further than she'd ever travelled.

On the road, Lyra felt an odd wetness.

"Stop for a minute," she called out. She dismounted and went to the roadside to pee. There was blood. She looked at Marie with a mix of dismay and confusion.

"You're a woman now," laughed Marie.

She helped Lyra deal with the blood, and as they rode through the mountains, she explained to the maiden what it meant to be a woman.

They followed the trail day and night, taking the best routes for the horses. Marie had packed more than enough food for the journey, and Lyra kept their water bottles filled. She kept thinking about seeing Joan again. She had nothing else to live for. She couldn't believe that the Free Zones were gone. She hoped that Androscoggin Free Zone was small enough to fly below the radar. She thought of Basquiat, and Glinda, and all the lovely people who lived there. She couldn't imagine them gone. Lyra was no stranger to loss and she gritted her teeth and turned her thoughts to Subhina, her baby sister.

She is who I live for now, thought Lyra. She forced herself to think of how to best keep Subhina alive, to avoid the pain of thinking of the people she loved who were now dead and gone from this world.

Marie was a great companion. On the journey, she told Lyra stories from books she had read. Marie was a tough and hearty woman with a bright spark in her eyes and a kind smile. She loved caring for the horses and she naturally became thick as thieves with Starlight and

Grease Lightnin. The dogs trusted Marie, just as Lyra did now.

They travelled through beautiful countryside, avoiding human interaction as much as possible. Instead of trying to get through one of the government checkpoints or the giant land border walls the Supreme Leaders had erected, Marie had the brilliant idea to forge the St. Croix River into Canada.

"It will drop us right into St. Andrews," she said. Joan's last documented location.

Lyra was nervous at the thought of crossing the large and powerful river, but it seemed better than trying to get through anywhere else, and the animals were like family to her. She couldn't bear leaving them behind, and she knew Marie wouldn't either.

They decided that it would be best for Marie to carry Subhina for the crossing. She wanted Lyra to focus on crossing the river safely. Marie had experience swimming with horses, and she was a far better swimmer.

Marie led the horses down to the riverbank. Lyra's horse stomped nervously and tossed her hair, picking up on Lyra's energy.

"Shh, shh," cooed Marie. "It's okay, this will be fun."

She led her horse into the river. Starlight and Grease Lightnin splashed in, fearless.

Lyra's heart raced. The river reminded her of that day she got swept away and Papa Gilles and Starlight saved her. A picture flashed in her mind of Papa Gilles' hand outstretched toward her as she clung for dear life to the log in the river. She still felt the ache of her poorly healed broken ribs, her bruised thighs, and Papa Gilles' face more scared than she had ever seen him in her life. She had an awful feeling that she was about to lose everything all over again-- her sister was going to be swept away by the river, and die right before her eyes, like the rest of her family…

"Lyra!" screamed Marie.

Lyra was slipping off the side of the horse. She was

passing out.

The sound of Marie's voice shook Lyra back to consciousness and she righted herself on the horse. The creature stomped with nervous relief, feeling Lyra starting to calm down.

By this time, Marie was already far out in the middle of the river.

"Come on," she shouted. "You can do this!"

Lyra looked at the tiny bundle in Marie's arms.

Subhina is fine, she told herself. *My sister is fine, everything is fine…*

She took a few long deep breaths.

This was it, and Lyra knew it. She stared hard at the river. There was no other choice.

Your sister is on the other side, she thought. *Marie is on the other side. Joan is on the other side.*

Lyra's future was on the other side. She turned to look back at the road they had taken to get here. She thought of her mother, Sayre. Tears pricked the edges of her eyes. She thought of Papa Gilles, and Brandon, and Inas, Basquiat and Glinda, and all the people of Dummer Mobile Home Park, the people she had met on her journey from child to woman.

She was ready. The horse felt it and proceeded into the waters of the St. Croix River.

CHAPTER 19: Lyra

Lyra and Marie arrived in St. Andrews. They were amazed at the friendly little city. There were no slums, nor were there palatial estates; the comfortable houses were cheerfully painted bright colours, with wild gardens, solar panels, and horses trotting through the streets.

"How do we find Joan?" asked Lyra.

"Maybe there is an arts district somewhere?" suggested Marie.

That made Lyra think of jam night at the Androscoggin Free Zone. Her thoughts involuntarily conjured up an image of people running screaming out of the old Megamart building, flames licking the mural she and Glinda had painted, and a road of bodies charred to a crisp. Lyra realized that she was hyperventilating and she forced herself to take deep breaths.

They are probably fine, thought Lyra. *They weren't harming anyone, they weren't challenging anyone... Their home was so much smaller than White Mountain Free Zone.* She hoped with all her heart they were just fine, making music and big delicious breakfasts, with their library and their growing garden.

Marie and Lyra made their way to the heart of the little green city. In the quaint downtown, there was an inviting-looking shop with huge windows. They peered inside and saw abundant and overflowing costumes, art supplies, posters, musical instruments and large tables set up in a massive light-flooded hall with artsy-looking folks of all ages working on something.

"Want to go in?" asked Marie, intrigued.

"Sure."

They hitched up the horses to the post outside, alongside the row of bicycles. When they opened the door, a friendly dog greeted them, wagging her tail. Starlight looked wary.

A little girl with two different coloured eyes galloped up to the door on a broom horse.

"Come on Haiku," she said, pulling the dog back to give them some room. She looked at the two unleashed dogs, then turned uncertainly inside.

"Onyx," she called.

An adult came over wearing a paint-covered apron. They had a smudge of paint on their eyebrow.

"You're welcome to bring the dogs in here, Haiku is very friendly," they said.

"Thank you," said Marie. She strolled in. Lyra and the dogs followed. Grease Lightnin and Haiku immediately started to chase each other around the huge space, knocking things off tables. Some of the artists in the room laughed.

"Haiku!" said Onyx sternly, and the dog slowed down, looking embarrassed.

"What brings you to the studio?"

Marie and Lyra looked at one another. *Where to begin?*

"Do you want some tea?" asked Onyx after a moment.

"Sure," said Marie with gratitude.

Onyx led them back to a kitchen area and fixed them some tea.

"You hungry?"

Marie and Lyra eyed the snacks on the counter.

"Take what you need."

Gratefully, Lyra grabbed some fresh fruit.

Onyx took them over to an area with some chairs and they sat down. They chatted pleasantly. Onyx explained that this was not a shop, but a community arts studio. They had reclaimed this formerly merchant space and de-capitalized it. Everyone was welcome here. Lyra and Marie explained where they had come from. Onyx listened patiently and attentively as they drank their tea.

"We don't want to take up all your time," said Marie apologetically. "You were obviously working on something."

Onyx laughed. "I am. But this break for tea is just what I needed, and your story is incredible." They smiled warmly and relaxed in the comfortable chairs, enjoying the moment. For the first time in a long time, Lyra felt safe. She looked around at all the people working on projects together, laughing and playing with puppets and various arts tools. The little girl with the broom horse was galloping around chasing the dogs. Teenagers were up on a balcony filming a video. There was a group of clowns practicing a skit. It was pandemonium, but in a fun and enticing way. She looked down at Subhina, wrapped up to her chest, who was sleeping peacefully through all of it.

"Joan was just here," said Onyx. "We supported one of her actions just a week or so ago. I'm afraid she is probably off on her next adventure by now though."

"You know Joan?" Lyra was amazed. Joan had left a trail of wonderful people for her to follow, from Soko, to Marie, now to Onyx and these wonderful artists. She felt like she was on a providential Joan pilgrimage, from holy person to holy person- but when would she meet the saint herself?

"She's drawn to places like this," said Onyx. "Places where future culture keepers are living the new paradigm."

"Like Marie's general store," said Lyra. "It was special like this too."

Marie nodded sadly.

Onyx smiled empathetically. "I'm sorry for what you've lost," they said.

"How will we catch up to Joan?" asked Lyra. "She travels so fast."

"Do you need a place to stay tonight?" asked Onyx quietly. "We have a live-work space here at the studio. I'm the current artist-in-residence, but we could squeeze you in if you need."

"Thank you. That would be lovely," said Marie.

Soon it was time for dinner. There was a huge pot of soup simmering away in the kitchen area. Some of the artists bid them farewell and went home for dinner, and others lined up with bowls for some nourishment to keep making late into the evening. One of the artists helped to find feed for the horses, and Marie, Lyra and Subhina stayed with Onyx in the apartment behind the studio.

The next day, Onyx helped Lyra to look into Joan's whereabouts. They messaged a fellow artist who knew Joan.

"Looks like she is headed to Cape Breton next," said Onyx. "There is a really cool intentional community there, called The Order. The place is called Gray House. It's the prototype for Snow Arcologies."

Valkyrie Snow's company, Snow Arcologies, a subsidiary of Hammer & Bone, was in the news a lot in recent years due to the success of Luna House, the arcology on the moon. There were arcologies popping up all over.

"Really?" asked Lyra excitedly. "I read that book, *The Art of Architecture*," she said.

"We have a copy here," said Onyx, gesturing to the shelves of books on one wall of the studio. "I brought it back when I visited. It's not that far from here."

Lyra pulled up a map online. It was quite far.

"Well relatively close by Canadian standards," laughed Onyx. "It will still be a trek by horse."

Lyra felt a tremor of purpose course through her. Although disappointed that they had missed Joan, Lyra felt that this was happening for a reason. They were meant to go to Cape Breton and see Valkyrie Snow, the brilliant artist who had dreamed up the arcologies and drawn them in sharp pencil.

Marie and Onyx had become fast friends. Onyx was fascinated with Marie's trading post general store and her bartering and self-sufficiency. They discussed how such a thing would work in an urban context. Marie was reluctant to leave, but she was committed to seeing Lyra realize her dreams.

Maybe we can come back here after, she thought.

Onyx and the community of artists helped their new friends prepare for the journey to Cape Breton. It felt much different than Marie's sad departure from her ancestral home.

"Thank you for your stories," said Onyx. "Please come back and visit us."

"I have a favour to ask you," said Marie. "Can I leave my tinsmithing tools here for safekeeping?"

Onyx laughed. "It's pretty packed in here. If you can find a good spot, you can leave them, but beware someone might use them!"

Marie considered. She expected that the people here would respect her tools, maybe more than anyone she had ever met. They were heavy for the horse, and she didn't want them damaged on the journey, especially since they needed to save space to pack food. She found a corner in the studio storage area and tucked them up securely.

"I would usually say no to that kind of responsibility, care-taking another artist's tools, but if it means you'll come back to us, I have to say yes." Onyx grinned and gave Marie a big hug.

Again, Lyra, Marie and Subhina set out on horseback, this time for Cape Breton, in search of Joan Whiteduck.

The journey was just as beautiful, but less scary than the first stretch had been. There were no roaming highwaymen with guns in Canada. Finally, the equestrian trail they were on brought them to a beautiful beach where smiling people were lounging around, enjoying the last warm days of summer. Two men strolled happily from the field to the beach holding hands. The tall one remarked at the horses and came over.

"Hello," he said loudly.

"Hello," said Lyra carefully. Her ratio of positive experiences with men favoured caution. She was ready to bolt if necessary.

The other man caught up and smiled shyly. For some reason, he made her feel more at ease.

"Will you be needing to stable these?" asked the tall man.

"You ran into the right person," said the other man with a quiet smile.

"Yes," said Marie. "Thank you."

"I'm Kip," said the tall man. "This is Ben."

The travellers followed Kip and Ben to the stables.

"What beautiful creatures," remarked Marie, checking out the horses in the nearby field.

"Thank you," said Kip.

They unsaddled the horses and let them roam in the enclosure.

"Let me take you up to the house," said Kip. "It's almost time for me to start making dinner anyway."

"See you later," said Ben, giving Kip's hand a squeeze and heading back up to the arcology.

As they followed Kip up a well worn path, Lyra felt like she was in a dream. The arcology rose high behind them. It was like a medieval citadel and some kind of futuristic alien structure at once, rising in a tall spiral.

The path before them was shaded by ancient trees, and they emerged into an open area with boxes and boxes of raised garden beds, fruiting trees and bushes, and clucking hens. There was a simple two-story blue-gray house with smoke curling from the chimney ahead. Off to the right, up a long laneway, was a tiny stone cottage.

"Lots of people live in the arcology, and in the village by the beach," said Kip. "But I still like Gray House better. This is where it all began, before the arcology was built."

Gray House used to be used as a living area but now it housed workshop space. They walked inside. Lyra loved the crooked old floors and furniture crammed into rooms that felt full of powerful energy. Many meetings and conversations which had led to great action took place here. Lyra ran her hand along the wall.

The kitchen was packed. People were chatting and listening to music as they peeled potatoes, chopped vegetables, and prepared the meal. Kip jumped right in to help out. Marie and Lyra followed suit. In no time they were laughing along too, including Subhina, who was being dangled in the air by an old man who loved babies.

At dinner, Lyra looked around the large screened porch filled with rows of tables where the community ate together in the summertime. There were many interesting faces, but not the one she was searching for.

"No Joan," she said with disappointment.

"I'm sorry," said Marie.

A woman with a big round belly squeezed onto the bench beside Lyra. Her eyes were on Subhina.

"Hello little one," she cooed, rubbing her own belly.

Subhina smiled.

"She likes you," said Lyra.

"May I?"

Lyra nodded as the woman gently picked up Subhina and held her close.

"I'm Octavia Dawn," said the woman, resting Subhina on top of her belly.

"Lyra, and this is Subhina. And that's Marie," said Lyra.

Marie smiled warmly.

"You must be due soon," said Marie.

"Just a few weeks before she meets the light," said Octavia.

"She? You're having a girl?"

"Yes."

"We know it must be a girl," said an older woman nearby, listening in and leaning over.

"How?" asked Marie.

"Because she is the First Mother," cackled the woman. "This baby was conceived through Octavia's will. Immaculate Conception."

"Well, sort of," said Octavia. "She wasn't conceived, really… but my doctor and I told her to be born. We told the egg to start gestating, the way you tell your lungs to hold your breath. Conscious thought exerting will over unconscious processes in the body… with communication made possible through nanites."

Lyra nodded. She didn't know what nanites were, except vaguely that they were scary government mind-control according to people like Old Jean, but she was not surprised that the people who built this citadel could harness the power of this special technology.

"Wow," said Marie. "Do you think I could do that?"

"Yes," said Octavia after a moment. "Any one who can make eggs has the building blocks of life in their body. You could be injected with nanites, but it's difficult to say exactly what the effect would be. I was born with them in my body, transferred from my mother to me, so I have had many years of training to bring this to fruition." Octavia's eyes flicked over to an elegant older woman at a nearby table.

Lyra followed her eyes and found that the woman was looking at them with interest.

"I am the first, but there will be others, after me."

The elegant older woman slipped over and sat down

across from Octavia. She reached out a hand. Octavia
took it.

"Lyra, Marie, Subhina," she said, using a sweet voice
when she said the baby's name, "this is my mother."

"Nice to meet you," murmured Marie.

Lyra looked into the woman's eyes. They were wells
of grey.

"I'm Valkyrie Snow," she said.

"You like sharp pencils," said Lyra quietly.

Valkyrie smiled. It was a rather rare expression on
her normally pensive face.

Lyra recognized the sharp line of her nose and chin
from the book jacket photo. The woman before her was
much older now, with many fine lines and silver curls, but
it was definitely her.

Suddenly, there was a commotion in the hall. News
spread fast, and soon it reached their table. A consortium
of nations led by Russia, China, and Iran had dropped
a series of nuclear bombs on major USA cities. The
Americans were able to deflect a few but not all of them.
The devastation was widespread. The mood in the hall
shifted and no one knew what to say.

Lyra and Marie were stunned.

A man got up from the table and fell backwards. He
was panicking.

"My father! My father is in Washington D.C…"

Someone tried to calm him and he swiped at them.
A woman stood from a nearby table, took several
swift strides toward him, and incapacitated him with
one graceful move. It was almost silent, the gentlest
takedown Lyra had ever seen. The woman knelt and
squeezed his shoulder affectionately. Lyra was deeply
impressed. She thought of the man at the abandoned store
who had ripped out her hair, and how defenseless she had
felt.

"Do you want to be like her?" said Valkyrie quietly,
observing Lyra's rapt expression.

Lyra turned to look at Valkyrie, annoyed at herself

for betraying her emotions so plainly.

"It's alright, I do too," said Val.

Reports about the loss of life and other damages rolled in over the following days. Lyra realized that if she had stayed in Dummer Mobile Home Park she would be dead.

Valkyrie summoned Lyra to her study. The room was at the top of the spiral tower. Lyra lingered in the doorway for a moment, unsure.

"Come in, come in," said the woman, without looking up from her work.

Lyra came over without making a sound. Shadows filled the corners of the room. She stood close enough to the woman to see what she was working on. A massive roll of creamy paper was laid out flat on a stone table bathed in light from above.

Good light, thought Lyra Muse, the artist.

Bold shapes drawn in crisp carbon were filled with ghost lines of miniscule detail. One large form depicted a polished vessel not unlike the design of the citadel itself. The master artist was adding fine detail to another image of a hangar deck with a smaller vessel nested inside. There was another sheet on the floor, partially rolled, depicting a half-finished circular room with many computer panels. Lyra's fingers itched to unroll the paper and inspect it closer, but she did not.

Valkyrie put down her pencil. The wood clattered softly on the stone table with a satisfying certainty.

"Mercury must help me with that one," said Valkyrie, gesturing to the incomplete piece on the floor. "She is a genius with computers. Exactly the mind I was longing to collaborate with. All this was possible because of her."

Somehow Lyra understood that the woman meant the arcologies.

"Why did you come here?" said the woman.

"I... I'm not sure," said Lyra. "I was looking for Joan, but she's not here."

"Sometimes people come here to run away from something. But sometimes they are looking for something… and those are the people who always find just what they need."

Lyra walked closer to the table, inspecting the drawings Valkyrie was working on.

"What is it?" she asked.

"It's a spaceship."

Lyra's eyes widened with recognition, then narrowed as she assessed the details more critically.

All this came from her mind, thought Lyra. *She is as crazy as I am.*

"So much art is a mere imitation of life and stops there," said Valkyrie softly. "There is art with another kind of truth to it, but it's commissioned by a decadent class on the verge of collapse but they don't know it… you can feel the listless anxiety in the shadows."

Lyra said nothing but she knew what the woman meant. Many of the popular artists on social media were not the ones Lyra found compelling.

"Art can be much more than that. Art can draw people into another world like nothing else can."

"I am an artist too," said Lyra finally.

"This is a good place for an artist," said Val. She tilted her head as though she were listening. "The Oracle says you are called Lyra Muse."

"I called myself Lyra Muse." She struggled to offer an explanation but no words came out.

"Snow was my own naming as well," said Valkyrie.

"Really?"

"I had a name. Then I had a married name. Then I had a divorce. Snow was moving forward."

Lyra circled the room slowly, taking in the drawings on the wall. Some were Valkyrie's and others were clearly other artists'. They were all pencil, charcoal, and ink.

"Do you think you will stay with us?" asked Valkyrie.

Lyra stopped with surprise. She had been running so long she had never considered staying anywhere.

"Maybe. But everyone here fits so well. I don't know where I fit."

"What about your baby?"

"My sister," said Lyra. Subhina was blissfully enjoying the daycare in the citadel and giving Lyra and Marie a break. Taking care of a baby was hard work. "She likes it here."

"I have someone I'd like you to meet."

There was a knock at the door. Valkyrie's timing was uncanny.

"Come in."

Lyra looked to the door to see the woman from the dining hall who had gracefully incapacitated the testerical man.

"This is Mika."

Mika approached.

"Mika, this is Lyra. I'd like her to apprentice with you, if she wants to."

Lyra looked at the two powerful older women before her. In Dummer Mobile Home Park, young women were treated like the property of men, and women who could no longer bear children were treated like ghosts. Lyra stood in the presence of not one, but two, formidable women who were quite possibly the strongest and smartest people she had ever met, and Lyra suspected there were many more in the citadel. She nodded solemnly.

"Your training begins today, then. Go with Mika. She will take good care of you."

Mika nodded and turned to leave. Lyra followed but paused at the doorway.

"Thank you for taking us in," she said.

"We are blessed when good people decide to be friends with us, Lyra Muse."

Lyra left the office of Valkyrie Snow following Mika Nakamura.

CHAPTER 20: Joan

The next morning, Joan Whiteduck awoke to find herself alone in the hotel room in St. Andrews. There was a handwritten note on the bedside table. Joan picked it up and scanned quickly to the bottom, seeing Apollo's name. She went back to the top and read through it slowly.

She dropped the note back on the table. Apollo had left. She had not one, but two boyfriends back home, and couldn't bring herself to tell Joan. She was embarrassed, and she left without saying goodbye.

Joan was stunned.

This was her first experience like this. As an only child of parents with successful careers, she was doted on her whole life. She never knew what a 'no' felt like, on a personal level, let alone an outright rejection. She was blindsided beyond her own capacity to understand. She let herself be devastated for a few minutes. She cried a little, and took a shower, letting the water wash away her pain. Joan was tough though. She had an important day ahead of her- maybe the most important day of her life so far. She could not let this confusing and hurtful experience take away what this day was for.

Joan made her way to the home of her mother's family bearing her mother's ashes. She had been here only twice as a child, and yet this family was etched into her core memories. They held each other as they went together to Aniapsuin's tomb.

Together they harvested clay from the river and mixed in her mother's ashes and red ochre. Joan sculpted a figure of her mother sitting, in the shape the elder told her was traditional for her mother's people, her people. As she adorned the figure with a birchbark shroud, Joan painted black marks on her face in the tradition of mourning, and finally, she let herself cry for her mother's spirit. The elders instructed the gathered community to build a pyramid over her mother's tomb. It was humbling and transformative. Joan felt that her journey in honour of Aniapsuin was finally complete. Although two years had passed since her mother died from cancer, Joan carried the pain every day. At last, she felt like her mother's spirit could rest.

That night, she called her father to tell him about the day.

"I'm happy for you," said James. He was also relieved that the long journey was over, and Joan would finally be coming home.

"Don't get excited yet Dad," said Joan. "Next I have to find my sister. I have to find Octavia."

"I know," he said. "But at least the dangerous protests are over."

There was silence on the line. "For now," Joan finally said.

When the call was over, Joan pulled out a velvet bag that she carried everywhere. She reached in and pulled out the wrinkled pages of the letter that Ania left her daughter on her deathbed. It contained advice, stories from their life together, cherished secrets and memories. Joan knew the words by heart and just holding the pages of the letter comforted her. There was one big surprise contained in the letter: Ania told Joan that she had a half-sister. James had fathered a child while he was working in the East on the famous arcology project. Soon after, he met and fell in love with Joan's mother and they moved back to the West. James wasn't even really sure if the first child was his, and Ania took his word for it and did not think much of it as they lived their lives with their little girl Joan. However, when Aniapsuin saw a picture of this first daughter, much later, as a grown woman, she knew. Ania wanted Joan to know she had a sister now that she was losing her mother.

I hope Octavia can love you as a sister, the letter said.

Joan stayed with her relatives for a few more days, and then they said an emotional goodbye. She would not let this much time lapse before she spent time with them again.

As Joan set off to find her sister, she felt strange.

Will she love me or will she hate me? thought Joan. That's how people always reacted to her. It was a bizarre existence. People either loved what Joan was doing, or they resented her for shoving their own inaction in their faces.

I wonder what she's like... Joan had seen pictures of Octavia, but it was hard to tell how someone truly was without being face-to-face.

Joan called an auto-bus, an electric self-driving vehicle, to take her to Gray House. The sounds of the city faded into silence as she made her way out to the countryside, down a winding highway. Rain began to fall as the sun went down. Joan watched the large drops roll down the window. The sound of rain on the moon roof was mesmerizing. She let herself fall into a trance.

Suddenly an image popped into her mind, unbidden.

Apollo, thought Joan, with a jolt of pleasure and sadness. She let herself linger in the memory of waking up together in the hotel room and finding one another…

hands, lips… Then the sting of betrayal made her shake out of it.

"Put her behind you," she muttered.

She's a coward for leaving without telling you the truth to your face, Joan told herself.

She turned her thoughts to the future, and to meeting Octavia. As she fell asleep for the long drive East, she dreamed of her sister, Aniapsuin's dying gift.

CHAPTER 21: Apollo

Apollo fled St. Andrews to see Artemis. Her twin knew her better than anyone ever could. Artemis was in Montreal.

I need you, texted Apollo.

Where are you? texted Artemis.

I'm at your place.

Meet me at La Banquise, I'm starving.

See you there.

Apollo made her way to the restaurant near Artemis' apartment. She ordered the special and waited.

"This show is falling apart at the seams," said Artemis, blustering into the restaurant.

Apollo stood and hugged her twin tight.

"Sorry, what?"

Artemis sighed. They were working on a three-performer dramatic comedy, and the other two actors were having artistic differences.

Apollo just listened, eating her poutine and drinking tea.

"But enough about me, what is this emergency of yours?" said Artemis finally.

"Honestly I just feel better sitting here hearing your voice," said Apollo.

Artemis rolled their eyes. "What's going on? Tell me."

The siblings were named after the mythological figures Apollo and Artemis. In the old stories, Apollo was a Sun god, and he rode his fiery chariot across the sky. His twin Artemis was the goddess of the hunt and wild things. Their moms, Mika and Mercury, had named one baby Apollo, and the other Artemis, but when they were very young, Apollo and Artemis decided to switch names. They insisted to all they met, and finally Mika and Mercury accepted it. Apollo became Artemis, and Artemis became Apollo.

Apollo told her twin about her surprise encounter with Joan Whiteduck, and what had transpired between them.

"Scandalous, you sound like me," said Artemis.

"I don't know how you do it."

"Do what?"

"Keep everything straight. I feel terrible."

"Why? What do you feel terrible about?"

"Not telling her about Ben… and Kip… I feel like such an asshole."

Artemis gasped. "Who is Kip?"

Apollo explained how her once simple monogamous relationship with Ben had gotten more complicated since they last saw each other.

"You have juicier gossip than I do right now," said Artemis. "And I have a girlfriend, a boyfriend, and I live with my ex!"

"Well I can't handle it."

"The key is communication."

Apollo rolled her eyes.

"Sweetie, I know you're the introverted twin, but you need to get better about talking about things."

Apollo squirmed. "I just never had a chance to bring

it up…”

“It’s basically just dishonest, and a cop-out, to pretend you didn’t have a chance to bring it up,” said Artemis matter-of-factly. “You owe that girl an apology.”

“Ugh, I know. But the crazy part is, I can’t stop thinking about her.”

Artemis laughed. “Okay, so when are you going to see her again?”

“I won’t, I won’t ever see her again.”

“You would seriously choose not to see her ever again rather than have an uncomfortable conversation? Po, that’s twisted.”

“It’s too late, I left her a stupid note… and now I absolutely can’t ever see her again.”

The twins finished their poutine and left the restaurant.

“How long are you around for?” asked Artemis.

“At least a week, please… then I can get back to my life. I can’t stay too long though, Octavia is due in less than a month and my boss will be needing help in the lab.”

CHAPTER 22: Lyra

Mika Nakamura's movements were like magic. Each
gesture was powerful and precise. Lyra's training so
far consisted of a daily practice of physical exercises,
meditation, and history and lessons through storytelling.
There were several girls and women in the dojo. Lyra
was among peers for the first time in her life. Marie came
one day, but found it was not for her. Marie had found
good friendships in the gardeners. It was late fall and
there was a great deal of work to be done for the harvest.

Mika was an excellent teacher. She had turned
out several formidable students in her decades in the
community. Lyra was very keen and Mika enjoyed
mentoring her. The girl was quiet and focused, far beyond
her years.

This year marked Mika Nakamura's 60th birthday.
The years slipped by and in the last few she felt her
body shifting. Some mornings she woke up with pain
in her lower back. Her eyesight wasn't what it used
to be. Her hits weren't as hard as they once were. But

she was happier than she ever imagined she could
be. Her children, Apollo and Artemis, were growing
into formidable adults. Apollo was an award-winning
scientist and Artemis was an accomplished artist. Mika
and her wife Mercury were more in love, with the deep
love that comes from years of mutual service and care,
than she ever thought possible too.
Lyra was quietly awed by Mika, and by Mercury too.
Mercury Elmahdy was Allat, the computer genius
who had inspired a generation of hackers called
Femnonymous to engineer gender chaos on the internet.
Mercury was the instigator, and the collective carried on
her great work. Lyra knew all about it because Joan had
posted about it online. Joan was inspired by Allat in her
activism. A whole new generation of youth were inspired
by Allat through Joan Whiteduck.

Mika and Mercury had two children, with the help
of fertility science blending their DNA. They were
pregnant together at the same time, but Mika's pregnancy
miscarried. Mercury gave birth to twins, who were named
Apollo and Artemis.

One day, Marie decided to leave the community and
return to St. Andrews.

"I miss my tinsmithing," said Marie gently.

"You could do it here," said Lyra, troubled at the idea
of missing Marie's presence in her life.

"You're right, I could. But remember the art studio in
St. Andrews? And Onyx? We've been talking, and Onyx
wants to help me open a barter shop next door to the
studio. It's got me more excited than anything since we
had to leave my grandmother's shop," said Marie. "I need
this."

Lyra searched Marie's face, struggling to accept this
difficult news.

What about Subhina? she thought. *What about me?*

Another child might cry or have a temper tantrum.
Lyra was no such youth.

"I understand," she said slowly and quietly, pushing down any urge she might have to react emotionally. "I'll miss you."

Marie's eyes welled up and she smiled and cried at once. She wrapped her arms around Lyra and hugged her tight.

"It's not that far," she said. "We'll visit each other, and I want to hear how you're doing all the time."

Lyra nodded and squeezed back with an iron grip.

Soon after Marie left, Valkyrie Snow called for Lyra, this time to her little stone cottage, a tiny building tucked away on the laneway up to the property.

Lyra opened the thick wooden door and stepped into the darkness inside.

"Hello?" she said.

"Hello," said Valkyrie softly from a rocking chair in the corner of the room. She gestured for Lyra to come take a seat at the plain wooden table. There were dusty unfinished drawings on the table and jars of partially sharpened pencils along the windowsill.

"What is this place?" asked Lyra.

"This is my house, my studio, my refuge, my birthing room, my rebirth," said Valkyrie with a touch of a smile, retreating into decades-old memories. "When I first imagined the Citadel arcology, out there on the empty beach, I lived here in this little stone cottage. I moved into the Citadel years ago and I haven't visited Stone Cottage since."

Lyra ran her finger through the dust on the table, and looked around in wonder. She looked back at Val, waiting to find out why she was here.

"I heard that Marie left The Order," said Val.

Lyra nodded, her expression impassive.

"I know you're taking care of your baby sister; are you doing okay?"

Lyra nodded again. It was hard, but she was managing. No alternative entered her mind.

"Please let me know if there's anything I can do to help you," said Val, gazing at her with a concerned expression. "I want you to know that this is your home if you choose it to be, and we will take care of you."

Lyra choked a quick rise of emotion down and nodded. Back in Dummer Mobile Home Park, she would have had to do terrible things to be taken care of.

"I've summoned you here because you are an artist, and you need a studio."

Lyra blinked several times, not comprehending.

"A Room of One's Own," said Val. "Over there is a little wood stove that will keep you warm in winter." She pointed to the stove. "Up those stairs is a loft with a comfortable little nook perfect for sleeping with a baby."

Lyra realized that Valkyrie Snow was offering her this cottage of stone to live in with Subhina. She couldn't say a word.

"You'll have to please let me know what kind of tools you'll need."

"Tools?" asked Lyra, finally.

"Tools. Brushes, paints? I heard you are a painter," said Valkyrie.

"Oh, yes..." said Lyra, still mildly stunned.

"I'll get you started. I expect to check in on you and see what you're working on," said Valkyrie. "It will be such a pleasure to watch you develop your practice."

"Thank you," said Lyra gravely and sincerely. "Can I ask you a question?"

"Of course."

"Is art really that important?" she asked. During hard times, Joan's bold art made her feel like the world could get better. But lately, with all the chaos happening in her homeland, the information on the news was just so heavy... She deeply respected Valkyrie Snow's opinion, and she knew the artist would understand the question.

"Art is essential for a community to exist," said Valkyrie. "We are the keepers of the dreams of our people."

Val tilted her head and her eyes became soft, as though she was no longer looking through them, but rather inside. She stood up abruptly and walked to the door.

"Do you have any more questions?" she asked. "Before I go?"

"You called this your birthing room, and your rebirth…" said Lyra.

This is where I gave birth to Octavia Dawn and became a mother," said Val.

"I have no mother," said Lyra. "No father, no family… except Subhina."

"I'm done being a mother… but I'm preparing for the great journey of being a grandmother to many, if you'd like to think of me like that." Valkyrie smiled at the idea. "This," she said, gesturing around the little cottage on her way out the door, "is where I dreamed a new future for myself, and was reborn into a new life of my own creation. Never believe that you can't make your dreams come true."

"That," said Lyra, "I have always known."

Lyra kept herself very busy cleaning the stone cottage and making it her own. She gathered together the items she would need and rearranged the cottage.

Reminds me of Papa Gilles' cabin.

The thought gave her comfort. She pulled out the smooth silver bird, the toy Lyra and Sayre had found in the dresser at the cabin, and placed it on the blanket on the floor for Subhina to find.

She carefully unpacked the rest of her precious satchel. She put the little punch-tin candle holder with the star pattern made by Marie at the centre of the table. Marie had given it to her the day they met, when Papa Gilles had taken her to Randolph General Store.

I'll have to learn to make some beeswax candles, thought Lyra.

She took out each item one at a time. Her homemade brushes, paint-making tools, the tiny doll, Papa Gilles' bone-handled gutting knife… the items brought on difficult memories but she was happy to have them in this new place. The empty satchel she hung on a hook by the door with a deep sigh. She sank into the rocking chair with a sense of calm she had not felt in a long time. The room was so still, and Lyra felt at home. The stone walls felt so safe and secure, unlike the trailer in Dummer Mobile Home Park that had burned in the fire.

I must keep Subhina safe, she thought.

Octavia was taking care of Subhina, but soon Lyra's sister would come to live with her.

I will be mother, sister, and family to you, she thought.

Lyra loved her mother Sayre. There were times when Lyra thought she was a bad mother, and times that she did not keep Lyra safe, but she never stopped loving her. Lyra squeezed her eyes shut, remembering the bad times. She resolved to do better. Did Sayre teach her anything good about motherhood?

She did her best, Lyra realized. *That's a lesson I can take from Sayre.*

The house was ready. Lyra had made the upstairs nook perfectly cozy for sleeping, and downstairs had the beginnings of an art studio.

Soon after, Octavia Dawn brought Subhina to the cottage. She lumbered inside, her belly so large and ready to pop.

"Soon Subhina will have a friend," said Octavia.

Lyra grinned with excitement. Subhina would have so many things Lyra herself could never have dreamed of having growing up. Subhina would have great friends in the little village school.

When Octavia left, it was just Lyra, Subhina and the dogs. It was strange to imagine that they would live here, in this little cottage, on an island in the East of Canada.

How weird life is, thought Lyra.

Under the tutelage of Mika, Lyra discovered that visual art was not her only passion. She loved martial arts. Painting fired up her mind, and fighting practice fired up her body. Somehow, her daily practice made her feel more in control of her own life and her own destiny than she had ever felt before. Mika was a true warrior, and Lyra respected her and trusted her with her life.

"What is your goal with your practice?" asked Mika.

"I want to face my enemies with strength," said Lyra, thinking of times she had been afraid for her life. "And I want to protect the people I love."

The circle of people Lyra loved had eclipsed, and now was growing bigger. There were so many kind people here. And one day, when she finally met Joan Whiteduck, she wanted to be able to protect her too.

CHAPTER 23: Joan

Joan's autonomous taxi arrived at its destination in the early hours of morning.

"You have arrived," said the calm robotic voice of the vehicle. It powered down in a long unlit laneway.

Joan looked outside. The trees glistened from the night's rain, in the darkness of early morning. She could make out a small house by the driveway, and the medieval, alien looking fortress in the distance that she recognized as the famous citadel arcology designed by Valkyrie Snow. She was excited that her sister had grown up in this interesting, counter-cultural place. Joan dared to hope that they would have some things in common. She wondered why the taxi had stopped here, and not up at the citadel. She squinted at a hand-painted sign in the ditch, and got out of the vehicle to see it better.

Welcome to The Order, it said.

Beside the road there was a charming little cottage made of stones. It was comically small, but solid and inviting, almost like something from a fairy tale. Joan took a moment to admire it.

Suddenly a face appeared in the window. Joan stepped back, startled. The heavy wood door opened a crack and a face popped out.

"What are you doing here?" asked a voice sharply.

"I… I'm looking for my sister," said Joan.

The door opened wider and the girl stepped out. Joan looked her up and down. She was barely a teenager. The girl's head cocked to one side, and she squinted.

"Are you… you look like… you can't be… Joan Whiteduck?"

Joan sighed with resignation. This was her life.

"Yes, I'm Joan Whiteduck."

"Come in, come in," beckoned the girl.

Joan grabbed her bag from the taxi and followed the girl into the stone cottage.

Inside the cottage was as charming as the outside. The furniture was simple and handmade. A little woodstove took up one corner, and a rocking chair the other. A table and chairs graced the centre of the room, and little shelves held papers, jars of various liquids and bits and bobs. An artist lived here.

The girl gestured to a chair.

"Your sister you said?" she asked.

"Um, yes," said Joan, sitting down. "Her name is… Octavia."

"Really? Octavia is your sister?" said the girl.

"Yes, I think so," said Joan. She couldn't believe this girl knew her sister.

A baby wailed from up in the rafters.

"Excuse me," said the girl, darting up wooden stairs by the door. She returned with a baby in her arms.

"My sister," smiled the girl shyly. "Subhina."

"And what's your name?"

"Oh. Lyra, Lyra Muse."

Joan was stunned. The sun was rising and she was tired from the long drive, and the girl with her baby sister in the stone cottage seemed so surreal.

"How do you know Octavia?" she asked.

"Octavia takes care of Subhina sometimes," said Lyra. "You know, because she's pregnant. It's good practice."

Octavia is pregnant? I'm going to be an auntie! thought Joan.

"Do you live here? In the cottage?" asked Joan, and then felt it was a silly question.

"Yea. We do."

Joan nodded but didn't ask further. Maybe their mother was upstairs.

'Sorry to barge in on you at this ridiculous time of the morning," said Joan.

Lyra grinned. "I don't mind," she said. She paused a moment, feeling suddenly shy. She didn't want to say what she was thinking: *Joan, you inspire me. I came here, from the world I knew, on the whim of meeting you again, and here you are...* "I... follow your work," she said. "I... I'm happy to meet you."

Joan was relieved to know it was a safe space. "Is this yours?" she asked, gesturing to an unfinished painting on the table.

Protect the Places You Love, it said, with a beautiful forest teeming with animals and life.

"Yes. It's about how we should fight to protect the places we love, or else they will be destroyed by war and climate change."

Joan nodded, looking more intently at the image. "Right on," she said, with a new appreciation for this Lyra Muse.

They chatted for hours as the sun rose, until a decent hour.

"It's almost eight," said Lyra. "Let's go up to Gray House for breakfast."

Outside, the taxi was long gone. Joan and Lyra and Subhina made their way up the gravel road to a big old house. People dressed in colourful clothes were making their way inside.

"This is Gray House," Lyra said. "Everyone in the Order comes here for meals together." She pointed down the road. "Over there is the Solar Village… travellers and students live there."

"What about the arcology?" asked Joan.

"That's where long-time community members live, leaders, elders, families," said Lyra. "There's a big mess hall in there, but people don't really eat there in the summer. It's so nice out here in the gazebo."

The gazebo was a giant screen porch full of tables and chairs off the summer kitchen. People were sitting around enjoying coffee and morning food.

"There's Octavia," said Lyra, pointing with a smile.

Joan felt like she was in a dream. There she was, the sister who had existed secretly, far away, her whole life. Octavia was glowing, her belly big and round. She looked unmistakably like James, Joan's father, but there was something else. Her hair was wild with soft large curls, and her chin was pointed.

Feeling their gaze, Octavia turned her eyes to Lyra and the young woman beside her.

Lyra waved and headed over, Joan behind her.

Joan felt her heart flutter as she approached Octavia. The words from her mother's letter played over in her mind.

Octavia reached up and took the baby from Lyra's arms. She cooed and cuddled her close.

"Good morning," she said.

Lyra smiled and looked at Joan with a question in her eyes, wondering if she needed an introduction.

"This is Octavia," she said matter-of-factly. "This is Joan."

"Um, hi,' said Joan, feeling silly, not knowing where to start. "Nice to meet you."

"I'm going to get a plate," said Lyra, excusing herself and heading to the summer kitchen where volunteers were assembling various breakfast foods.

Joan started with her mother's letter. Right there, in the gazebo filling with breakfast eaters, she told Octavia everything she could about why she believed they were sisters. They chatted happily. Joan felt a bond with this woman that she never expected. As an only child, she never imagined she would have this kind of feeling with another person in this lifetime. Conversation flowed easily between them, like their separate upbringings were just a temporary disconnection.

Lyra sat quietly across from them, eating her breakfast and listening to the story, in awe that this was Joan Whiteduck.

Suddenly, Octavia felt a twinge of sharp pain in her abdomen. She gasped at the force of it, like nothing she had felt before.

Joan's smile died on her lips, her face shifting from joy to concern.

"Octavia? Are you alright?"

Octavia's eyes were wide with the realization that the time had come.

"It's… I'm… I think it's happening," she said quietly. "It's happening," she said louder, looking around. Lyra looked up in alarm.

"Mika," she called. She scanned the gazebo and locked eyes with Mika, who took a quick step forward, jumped over the long table between them, and with one more quick step she was by Octavia's side.

"Is it time?" grinned Mika, holding Octavia's back firmly. "Let's get you to the citadel."

Octavia thrust Subhina into Lyra's arms, and clutched her huge belly, with Joan and Mika supporting her on either side.

Around them, other people enjoying breakfast began to take notice of what was going on.

"Go," said Mika. "Tell Valkyrie. Get the doctor."

They made their way down the footpath to the towering arcology. Joan gripped her sister's hand, both nervous and reassuring. Again she felt the overwhelming sensation of the experience being surreal.

Octavia doubled over in pain with a moan.

"We should get you a car," said Joan with concern.

Octavia looked up the path to the arcology, still a ways to go. "I can do it," she said with determination.

"That's it," said Mika, pulling her up and continuing.

A few steps from the door, Valkyrie burst out.

"Mumma," cried Octavia, falling into open arms. Valkyrie squeezed her tight.

"Come, come," she said, pulling her daughter inside. "It's time!"

They laughed and cried as the contractions grew stronger, hurrying down the grey stone hallways with soft light until they reached the medical theatre.

The doctor arrived soon after.

"Here we are," she said.

A man appeared in the doorway. He had a ponytail and his unshaven chin was flecked with silver.

"Come, darling," beckoned Valkyrie softly. "We will be grandparents soon."

Jordan Barker came in and kneeled beside the bed, peppering Octavia's hand with kisses.

"It's happening, Daddy," said Octavia, laughing.

"You've got this, baby girl," he said, his voice choking. His eyes were misty.

Octavia laboured for hours. Valkyrie, Jordan, and Lyra took turns comforting her. Joan sang the Honour Song, in the tradition of her people. This experience reminded her deeply of the death ceremony for her mother. Life and death were so closely linked. The death of one mother, and the birth of another…

Valkyrie was wiping sweat from her daughter's brow. Jordan and Lyra sat in chairs by the door.

"So who is that?" whispered Jordan to Lyra, gesturing to Joan.

"It's Joan Whiteduck," said Lyra.

"Oh. The artist?" Jordan, Valkyrie's partner, was a retired musician and he followed the contemporary art scene.

"Yes," said Lyra. After a moment, she added, "she's Octavia's half-sister."

Jordan was stunned. He blinked a few times, trying to connect the dots.

There had been moments he suspected he was not the biological father of Octavia Dawn. There had been hints over the years… but he chose not to think about it because he really disliked Val's ex-husband, and thought she might be his.

Jordan had wholeheartedly raised Octavia as his daughter. When she was born, he was in trouble. He was on a dark path. Caring for Octavia had saved his life, so he chose to be her father without question. This moment, however, was one of those bare-faced reminders of the mysteries of Valkyrie Snow.

He looked at the women holding his daughter's hands as she laboured, studying their features. Octavia had her mother's chocolate curls, and something else. Joan tilted her head, and there it was… the unmistakable traces of resemblance. Octavia Dawn had a sister. A sister with the same biological father. Jordan looked at Valkyrie, thinking of all those years ago when she herself had given birth.

Valkyrie felt his eyes speaking volumes across the room. She looked up, gazing at him with her eternal impassive expression.

He couldn't look away.

Valkyrie's lip curled ever so slightly into a smile.

Octavia let out an intense cry.

Finally, like Joseph, while Mary was giving birth to baby Jesus, Jordan looked away.

The baby came with labour but without crisis. Soon she was nestled into Octavia's arms, and the room, once so loud, was filled with hushed reverence.

"Do you have a name?" asked Lyra, holding Subhina, who suddenly seemed so big compared to the fresh little baby in Octavia's arms.

"Quinn," said Octavia. "I've decided to call her Quinn."

"Who is the father?" asked Joan. Everyone looked at her, and her cheeks tinged red as she realized that it might be an insensitive question.

"She is a miracle," said Valkyrie quietly.

"Immaculate Conception," laughed Octavia. "By my own will."

"What they mean is, a scientist figured out a way for Octavia to get pregnant through her own thoughts," said Lyra matter-of-factly. "With nanites and AI."

"No sperm needed," said Jordan Barker. "The egg has all the power it needs to become a baby. The sperm just sets the egg's process going… but the nanites can do that part. There is nothing the sperm contributes, just flips the switch." Somehow, saying it out loud made him feel less strange about Valkyrie getting her switch flipped by someone else.

"That's amazing," said Joan. "But what about… DNA?"

"Quinn, my granddaughter, and your niece, has nothing spliced into her that her mother did not already have. She is created from Octavia Dawn," said Valkyrie.

Joan let the information sink in. The revolutionary implications were enormous.

"My precious niece," she said, stroking Quinn's beautiful little cheek.

People with reproductive systems had all the tools necessary to grow a child. Until now, sperm cells were usually required to trigger an egg's development into a baby, but a genetically simple AI-enabled nanite fix allowed wombed-humans to trigger development themselves. As far as scientists could tell, sperm cells did not contribute anything to egg development, they simply carried a DNA profile.

As part of her research, Dr. Crystal's team trained Octavia Dawn's nanites to trigger egg development, and humans officially joined the other creatures that could reproduce via parthenogenesis.[2] In the future, women would be able to simply ask the Oracle to interact with their nanites and trigger pregnancy. This was essential research, because scientists realized in the early 2000's that Y chromosomes were evolving out of all species on Earth. If all humans were eventually to be females, these people would need to evolve a way to trigger reproduction.

At 29 years old, Octavia Dawn would be the First Mother to carry a parthenogenetic child in this method. She would be supported by The Order and the whole community. Children born here were nurtured by many, so that future generations would flourish, but child-bearers could continue with their lives and education if they wished. This was how The Order planned to sustain a new generation.

Octavia looked exhausted but triumphant. Her cheeks were glowing with life. She and Joan locked eyes with wordless smiles. Although they had just met earlier that day, they were bonded in blood, and now by the incredible experience that they had just shared. Joan's heart was fuller than it had been in a long time.

I am an Auntie, she thought.

---

[2] "Parthenogenesis is reproduction without fertilization, an ovum developing into a new individual without fertilization by a sperm" (Wake 2018).
"Parthenogenesis is the development of offspring from unfertilized eggs. Parthenogenesis forms a regular part of some sexual life cycles, but there are also many lineages of animals that have given up sexual reproduction and become obligately parthenogenetic" (Normark 2013). Many moss-dwelling tardigrades (Water Bears) reproduce asexually through parthenogenesis. Perhaps the most famous examples of parthenogenesis in popular culture are the story of the Virgin Mary, and Buddha's mother conceiving him in a state of blissful meditation under a banyan tree.

CHAPTER 24: Joan

Joan spent the next week revelling in the mosaic of life's intrigues. Her sister Octavia was grateful for the company, but when she needed rest and privacy, Joan stayed with the young artist, Lyra, in the stone cottage. It turned out that Lyra was taking care of her baby sister by herself. She was amazed to hear Lyra's life story, and all that had transpired since the day they had crossed paths at the Randolph General Store. She was sorry to hear that the people of the mountain were not successful in stopping the dam project that poisoned their water.

"I don't understand why they didn't listen to you," said Lyra crossly. "How can people be so stupid?"

"I don't know," said Joan. She herself couldn't fathom why people would act against their own long-term interests.

"Do you think one day we'll get there, and all be able to work together? For a better future?"

"I hope so."

They both sighed like two old women far beyond

their years.

"Well," said Lyra, after a while. "What's next?"

"What do you mean?"

"What are we doing next? Or I mean, you, but… I'm with you now Joan. I believe in you. I want to help you."

Joan smiled. The girl had said it with such pure generosity. Sometimes all the negative feedback made her forget that what she was doing meant something, to someone.

"Sometimes I feel like it's all for nothing, you know…" she said.

"Oh no," said Lyra. "No you can't think that way." She remembered something Glinda had said to her. "When you have an artist's heart, you have to make your art. You never know who it's going to touch, or what it's going to inspire."

Joan was surprised to feel tears at the edges of her eyes. She couldn't speak.

"You inspire me, Joan. You've inspired me my whole life. I want to help you."

"Well then," said Joan, finally. "Let's dream up something wild."

Lyra insisted that Joan properly meet Valkyrie Snow.

"Octavia's mother?" asked Joan.

"Yes. I think you should. I don't know why, I just think you should."

"Sure."

Joan arranged a visit to the top of the citadel. It was a large circular chamber built of stone. The walls were adorned with artworks in pencil and ink, in various shades of greys, blacks and sepia tones.

A woman with a mass of grey curls was standing at a large stone table in the centre of the room, light pouring down on her workspace. There were giant rolls of cream paper laid out and pinned down with fist-sized crystals on the floor around the table. As Joan approached, she could see drawings of different components of a vessel, one which looked something like the arcology, taking shape.

"You're designing a submarine?" she asked. "Or, wait… is it a spaceship?"

Valkyrie broke her concentration and looked up at Joan.

"Yes," she said.

Joan walked closer, stepping between the drawings.

"Joan Whiteduck," said Val. "You are James' daughter."

"Oh, yes," said Joan. She wasn't sure what else to say.

"James was a lovely man," said Valkyrie. She looked at Joan as though critically analyzing her features, looking for James, and thus the other part of her own daughter.

Joan nodded.

"And you're an artist."

"Yes."

Valkyrie turned back to her work and scribbled something.

"Well, I can see you're busy…" said Joan. "Lyra wanted me to come and see this amazing studio…"

"Yes. Lyra is quite captivated by your work."

"She is very supportive, yes…"

Valkyrie tilted her head, listening to a voice Joan couldn't hear.

"The Oracle says that the President down in USA is calling you a terrorist."

"Doesn't sound like I'll be visiting there again," said Joan wryly.

"He is comparing you to Allat."

"Well that's flattering," said Joan.

"She is safe here, as you will be if you choose to stay."

"Allat lives here? With The Order?"

"Yes. Allat is helping me design this ship." She gestured to the drawings.

Joan's eyes lingered on the drawings stretched out

across the floor. This was certainly an intriguing place.

"I can stay here a while," said Joan, "but I have to continue my work."

"Of course," said Valkyrie. She set down her pencil and walked slowly around the giant table. "The Oracle says you are very busy."

"The Oracle," said Joan. "I've heard of that. It's an AI that's a part of you now, right? The early one, the one designed by Martha Robena, without ads…"

"Yes. Many were destroyed, but the Oracle lives on in my body, and Octavia's, and now Quinn's…"

AI technology was invented by a scientist for the woman she loved, but under capitalism, every invention, good or evil, was twisted and contorted to make money. This was why Valkyrie insisted that she would only design arcologies for Mars if they were owned, operated, and controlled by the residents themselves, and not some trillionaire tech Meth. [3] The nanite AI prototype was too real, and too rogue to be profitable, so it was abandoned for versions engineered to make money with ads, and thus not contributing to positive development or improvement in the world whatsoever. The Oracle's nanite fog was inside of Valkyrie Snow, and her daughter Octavia Dawn was born with them. Octavia had an even deeper connection with the nanites, and an uncanny ability to consciously harness their access to her body's unconscious processes. One could also assume that Quinn would also have this ability…

"Quinn is so perfect," said Joan. "I never thought I would ever have a sister, let alone a niece."

"Oh yes. Who knew that a woman who was once barren will be the grandmother of so many?" said Valkyrie. "We are family now, Joan. You always have a place here, no matter where you go. And the work you're doing aligns well with our purpose here."

"Thank you. I'm not sure though."

"Not sure? What do you mean?"

"Well the way you live is amazing… the way you

make your own food, and produce energy, recycle waste, and all that, I love it."

"Yes? Go on."

"What about Land Back?"

Valkyrie tilted her head, which Joan came to realize was her absorbing information from the Oracle.

"Yes," said Valkyrie, finally. "Yes I see your point." She still looked lost in thought. "I can build arcologies, but there are other things I cannot do. That would be better suited to Allat."

Joan smiled thinking of how Allat would tackle Land Back.

"I think it's time that you met Allat."

[3] The 'Meth' reference is an ode to Richard K. Morgan's novel *Altered Carbon*. "Meths, named after the long-lived biblical character of Methuselah, are individuals with extended lives granted to them by re-sleeving [re-incarnating] regularly. The individuals in question are usually the wealthiest citizens, such as Laurens Bancroft. Laurens was, at his introduction, the oldest living Meth at three-hundred-and-sixty years old."

CHAPTER 25: Joan

Joan walked down the long corridor from the elevator
where Valkyrie Snow told her to get off. Each door was
decorated differently. Some had family photos, a nice
message, or a painted mural. Joan paused at one door,
covered in hand-cut collage art. She looked down the
hallway at all the different doors, and thought of all the
floors in the arcology.

A lot of people live here, she realized.

It was a pretty great setup, if you liked living in
community with other people. No bills, no toughing
it out alone. The arcology produced its own electricity
and temperature control through the methane gas from
humans and animals, wind power, and solar. There was
a community theatre group, art studio, medical facility,
and sophisticated production of organic food. Residents
contributed according to their skills and desires. And if
you cared about life on earth, it was carbon zero with no
negative ecological footprint. Joan was impressed. These
people were living what she preached.

Joan reached a door painted with a sun and moon tucked together. Number 212. She knocked. Soon, the door opened and a beautiful middle aged woman appeared.

"Hello?" she said with a polite but friendly smile.

"Hi, I'm Joan. Octavia's sister…. Valkyrie said I should come and meet you."

The woman beckoned her inside.

"Tea?" she asked.

"Sure."

The women sat together and chatted. They connected instantly. Mercury Elmahdy was familiar with Joan's work.

"You're incredibly brave," she said.

"That's funny coming from you," said Joan. "You're legendary."

They both were the kind of people who understood that someone had to do something, and took it upon themselves to do it. Mercury, as the online persona Allat, had kickstarted a paradigm shift in the digital world. The internet began as a place where information was supposed to be free and equalizing, but capitalism twisted its potential into merely an advertising billboard for large companies. After Allat made her move, hackers got more aggressive about putting the digital realm back into the hands of people.

"What's your next move?" asked Mercury.

"I'd like to do something big, like you did," said Joan. "I'm not sure what yet."

"Well when you figure it out, let me know. I'd like to help you."

Joan could hardly believe it.

Allat wants to help me, she thought.

There was a knock at the door.

"Excuse me," said Mercury. She went to the door.

A young woman walked into the room.

Joan blinked. She blinked again. She couldn't believe her eyes.

Apollo.

It was the woman from the hotel at the community arts action in Qonasqamkuk. The woman Joan had shared an intimate experience with who then disappeared. Apollo looked equally stunned to see her.

"I… ah… er…" stumbled Apollo. She seemed tongue-tied.

She looks embarrassed, thought Joan.

"Do you two know each other?" asked Mercury.

Joan said nothing. Her lips were shut tight. She crossed her arms.

Let's see what she has to say, thought Joan.

Apollo's mouth dropped open and she looked from one woman to the other. She took a step backward as if she was going to turn and run.

"Are you okay Apollo?" asked Mercury, confused.

There was a long and awkward silence.

"What are you doing here?" said Apollo finally, choking on her words slightly as though she were nervous. There was something in her voice… It sounded like hope.

Joan looked her up and down. *Did she follow me here?* she thought. She couldn't decide if it was romantic or psychotic. A mix of feelings rose up inside her; anger was there, certainly, but also an annoying warm attraction. She felt red rise in her cheeks.

"How did you find me?" she asked carefully.

"How did I… find you?" repeated Apollo, her cheeks equally red.

"Do you… know each other?" asked Mercury.

"Hardly," said Joan sharply, thinking of Apollo's pathetic goodbye note. Then she thought of their last moments together, Apollo's full lips… and she flushed again. She frowned.

"Um, yes mom," said Apollo, "yes we know each other…"

"Mom?" said Joan. "This is your mom. So you're just coming home, you had no idea I was here… great."

Joan turned to Mercury. "I have to go. I'm sorry. I'll come back some other time." She cast a glance at Apollo. "Or not. Or… depends. But I have to go."

She bustled over to the door.

"Goodbye," she hissed, as she passed Apollo. "Goodbye. See, it's not so hard to say it to someone's face."

Joan shut the door abruptly behind her.

CHAPTER 26: Apollo

"What was that all about?" blurted Mercury, after Joan had left.

"Nothing mom, it's… I don't want to talk about it."

"Like hell you don't want to talk about it. Tell me everything!"

"I…" Apollo thought of the time she spent with Joan. A mix of guilt, shame, and intense pleasure filled her.

"I can't talk about it."

"Don't be so dramatic. Just tell me."

Apollo didn't have the words.

"What did you do to her?"

"Mom! Why are you taking her side? You don't even know what happened!"

"Well then tell me! Something obviously happened!"

"Why was she here?" asked Apollo. "Was she looking for me? What did she ask about me?"

"She's an activist, Apollo. We talked about activism."

Apollo furrowed her brow.

"How did she know where to find you?"

"Val sent her over here. Now you tell me what's going on. Right now."

Apollo told her mum about her trip to St. Andrews. She tried to stay light on the details, but Mercury understood the situation immediately.

"Apollo my girl, you've got yourself in a pickle, haven't you."

Apollo's lower lip quivered. She tried to blink back tears.

"Oh come now," laughed Mercury warmly, pulling Apollo in for a hug. "My baby girl. Everything will be fine. You need to decide what you really want."

Apollo said nothing. *I want it all,* she thought. She wanted Ben, and Kip, and Joan too. She sniffled in her mother's embrace.

"Do you know what you want?"

Apollo nodded slightly.

"Well there! That's the hardest part. Now you need to go fight for what you want, even if it's hard."

Apollo said nothing, lingering in her mother's embrace.

"And whatever you do, you need to go apologize to that girl."

CHAPTER 27: Joan

Joan stormed away down the hall, completely caught off guard by the surprise. She never expected to see Apollo again.

And she's Allat's daughter. Perfect... she thought, thoroughly annoyed.

I should never have gotten involved with anyone in the first place.

She marched into the elevator.

"Wait!"

Joan looked up and saw the face of Apollo just as the doors closed. She crossed her arms.

"Hmph."

The elevator whooshed down to the ground floor. The doors opened.

Joan stepped out. She hesitated.

What should I do now? she thought. Joan was mad at Apollo, but she intended to be friends with Allat. She started walking, slowly, to the front door.

It would probably be good to be on good terms, she

thought. She slowed to a stop, letting her hand linger on the exit door.

The elevator doors opened behind her.

"Joan! Please, wait," said Apollo.

Joan frowned and turned around slowly.

"I'm waiting," said Joan. "Please, say what you need to say so I can go."

"I'm sorry," said Apollo. "I'm so awkward… I'm the most awkward person on the planet."

Joan couldn't help but smile slightly. Apollo was so awkward, and it was at least a little bit endearing. She felt her anger thaw.

"Honestly it's fine, and I don't want to be mad at you. Let's please just put this behind us."

"I didn't mean to hurt you," continued Apollo.

Joan felt her anger flare up again. "Grow up," she snapped. Then she took a deep breath to calm herself. "What you did was obviously hurtful, so please don't say you didn't mean to hurt me. Just stick with the apology."

"I'm so, so sorry," said Apollo. "I am truly sorry. And sorry for making excuses."

Joan looked into Apollo's eyes. The apology seemed sincere.

"Alright. I accept your apology." She turned back to the exit door.

"Joan, wait," said Apollo softly.

Joan turned her head.

"I… thank you, for accepting my apology. Thank you. Can we… Can I make it up to you somehow?"

"What do you mean, you want to be friends? I don't know if I'm ready for that, to be honest."

You really had me fooled, thought Joan. *I fell for it stupidly fast. I'm definitely not ready to be friends.*

"Actually… actually I'd like a second chance. I've been thinking about you since I left. I would love to start over with you if you'd give me a chance."

Joan's mind reeled. She turned her whole body to face Apollo, looking her up and down, remembering her soft skin, her strong arms, her gentle kiss. Then she remembered the note.

"What about your boyfriends?" asked Joan, seriously.

"I've lived with Ben for 4 years, we've been together for 5. We live here in the arcology. He's sweet, I think you'd like him."

Joan just looked at her, expressionless.

"And Kip… he came to the community recently and we just hit it off. He's not like Ben, he's more… fiery. We started hanging out, and he's been sleeping over at our place a lot. It seemed like it would be complicated, but it's actually not. We all get along really well."

Apollo stepped closer. She reached out and held Joan's hand. Joan did not pull away.

"Okay… so what do you want from me?"

Apollo's cheeks blushed crimson. "I mean, I'd like whatever you want to share. I would like to be your friend, your lover, both, or… just hear what you want."

Joan was stunned. This was definitely not like any proposition she'd received before. She looked down at her hand in Apollo's. She felt warm, and safe.

"I don't like that you lied to me…" she said.

"I hate that I didn't tell you about all this before. I wanted to, so many times… but I just couldn't bring myself to do it."

"You're a coward," said Joan. The words were harsh, but there was no edge to her voice. It wasn't playful, but it was almost friendly.

"Not everyone is a warrior like you," said Apollo with a little grin. "You're so brave…" They locked eyes and Apollo leaned toward her. Joan could feel her energy reaching out. She pulled back slightly.

"You led me on… you let me believe I could trust you," said Joan. "I don't want to get hurt."

"I know. I understand. I suck at talking about my feelings, but I'm going to try to do a better job, okay?"

Joan looked her square in the eyes.

"We'll see," she said.

"Thanks for giving this a chance," said Apollo, giving her hand a squeeze.

"Sure. Let's get to know each other a little, okay?"

They both laughed.

Apollo drew Joan into her arms for a big hug. Joan relaxed. It felt good.

"So what are you doing now?" said Apollo, after a long embrace. "You want to come over tonight?"

"Like you mean to your house with Ben and Kip?"

"Yea."

"I'm not ready for that yet," laughed Joan. "But, ya, actually. Yes. Eventually."

Epilogue: The Order

The topmost chamber of the arcology, the stone crown that was Valkyrie Snow's studio, was bathed in the low flickering light of a hundred candles, held by a hundred community members. The leaders were gathered together for a special ceremony of initiation for Lyra Muse. Lyra was beaming, with Joan and Octavia standing beside her.

As the people assembled, Valkyrie stood beside Mercury.

"What do you think of this 'Joan'?" she murmured in her silken cloak.

"I believe she is the voice of the next generation of Mothers," said Mercury, looking at Lyra's adoring face.

An image popped into Valkyrie's mind of Joan on the crucifix, naked, in a sea of angry voices, her face steely with a look of resolve.

A Mother in the making, she thought.

"I trust you in all things."

Lyra was so happy that her face hurt from smiling. Mika Nakamura, Lyra's great teacher, led the ceremony. Marie was there, visiting from solarpunk Qonasqamkuk where Onyx was helping her get a barter and tinsmithing shop going. She was snuggling Subhina tight.

Surrounded by community, Lyra thought of her long journey to get to this place where she felt peace for the first time she could remember. In her short life she had experienced great sadness and endured hardship beyond her years, but finally, finally, her tiny boat on the wide and stormy sea of life had landed on safe shores.

The ceremony was a glorious blur of emotion. Mika put a locket around Lyra's neck, and the ritual was complete.

The gathered candle-bearers moved in a circle, each taking their turn to speak to Lyra, the newest initiate in The Order. Each one she had met at least in passing before, but now their conversation held deeper meaning.

"We are family now," someone said to her, clasping her hands in theirs.

We are family now. Lyra felt it deep in her soul. *We are family.*

Octavia's smiling face was next.

"Welcome, Sister, to The Order," she said, smiling with pride.

Joan, beside her, felt a twinge of curiosity at the word Sister; it was a word she was contemplating a lot lately.

As the gathered left, they blew out their candles, and the room was getting dark. Lyra's close friends were clustered around, waiting until the very end.

Joan was next, and last to congratulate Lyra.

"I'm happy for you," said Joan. "This place is full of love, and you're going to be so cared for here."

Lyra put her arms around Joan.

"Thank you for inspiring me to come here," said Lyra. There were tears in her eyes. "Thank you for inspiring me to go on living."

Joan felt her lip quiver. The candles, the cloaks, and

the peculiar and special energy of this place got to her. The ritual opened her heart wide, and she cried too.

Valkyrie appeared beside them.

"Would you say a toast, Joan?" she asked.

They made their way around the large stone dais in the centre of the room. Small cups of elderflower kombucha were passed around.

Joan looked at the people around her.

"This place has the magical ability to make you feel at home," she said. "I came here with no idea what I was getting myself into."

She reached out and clasped Octavia's hand tight.

"I have a sister."

She looked at the tiny babe in her sister's arms. "I have a niece," she said with wonder.

"I have a lover," she said thickly, looking at Apollo with an intensity that made her lover flush. Her eye caught Kip and Ben standing nearby.

"I have three lovers," she said with a grin. Apollo flushed deeper red.

Mercury snickered.

"I have mentors." Joan smiled appreciatively at Mercury, Mika and Valkyrie.

"And I have a friend for life." Joan grabbed Lyra's hand and squeezed it.

"To Lyra, the bravest of us all," she said, raising her cup. "And to community."

"To Lyra, and to community!" they responded.

BIBLIOGRAPHY

Daly, Mary. 1973. *Beyond God the Father: Toward a Philosophy of Women's Liberation.* Beacon Press, Boston.

Fadden, Ray Tehanetorens. 1993. "They Lied to You in School: A Talk by Ray Tehanetorens Fadden." *Woodstock Museum,* Woodstock, New York.

Normark, B.B. 2013. "Parthenogenesis." in *Brenner's Encyclopedia of Genetics, 2nd ed.* eds. Stanley Maloy and Kelly Hughes. Academic Press.

Paul, Daniel N. 2022. *We Were Not the Savages - First Nations History, 4th ed.: Collision Between European and Native American Civilizations.* Fernwood Publishing, Halifax, Nova Scotia.

Wake, Marvalee H. 2018. "Modes of Reproduction Verts: Hermaphroditism, Viviparity, Oviparity, Ovoviviparity." in *Encyclopedia of Reproduction, 2nd ed.Volume 6,* p. 18-22.

Woolf, Virginia. 1929. *A Room of One's Own.* Hogarth House.

Xaintongeois, Champlain. 1613. *Les voyages du Sieur de Champlain Xaintongeois, capitaine ordinaire pour le Roy, en la marine.* Paris, chez Jean Berjon. https://www.canadiana.ca/view/oocihm.90024/3

QUINN'S REBIRTH

Chapter One: Quinn

Quinn's shoulders felt heavier with each step and her head pounded with a migraine that had lasted for days. She was almost there. The air was thick as mists from the sea met the dusty fumes of the wasteland. She resisted the urge to lick her

sore lips, crusty with dirt and salt.

Turning her face up to the sky, she frowned at the circling gulls whose calls rang out against the crashing of the surf along the shore. The sound was annoying, but the outline of birds against the grey sky was a welcome sight after days of walking through the wasteland.

A massive ring etched into the coarse grass came into focus. She walked to it. Stepping over its edge, her legs felt weak. She swallowed down the feeling tumbling around in her stomach and rising in her throat that felt like the universe sweeping her away. The overcast sky melted into a solid wall of stone rising up into the fog.

To be continued...

www.ingramcontent.com/pod-product-compliance
Lightning Source LLC
Chambersburg PA
CBHW052355030726
47599CB00014B/1080